# Soul Map

## Channeling, Art, and Self-Realization

### Nancy Winternight

Epigraph Books

Rhinebeck, New York

*Soul Map: Channeling, Art, and Self-Realization* ©2023 by Nancy Winternight

All rights reserved. No part of this book may be used or reproduced in any manner without the consent of the author except in critical articles or reviews. Contact the publisher for information.

ISBN: 978-1-960090-01-0

Library of Congress Control Number: 2022923248

Book design by Nancy Winternight

Epigraph Books

22 East Market Street, Suite 304

Rhinebeck, NY 12572

(845) 876-4861

epigraphps.com

# *Soul Map*
## *Channeling, Art, and Self-Realization*

## Table of Contents

Introduction: The Questions

| | |
|---|---|
| Chapter 1: Channeling | 7 |
| Chapter 2: George, the Grandmothers, & the Angels | 31 |
| Chapter 3: Teaching and Expressive Arts | 59 |
| Chapter 4: Self as Artist | 81 |
| Chapter 5: Balance, Integration, Synthesis | 88 |
| Chapter 6: The Energy Mandalas | 101 |

# Introduction: The Questions

A former Expressive Arts student sent me an email, asking me how I got started in Expressive Arts. I realized when I began my response to her that it wasn't going to be short. Along with my answer, I included my website, which lists channeling angelic energy among other things. This sparked a second question from her regarding communicating with angels. This time, my response turned into a book.

How does one tell one's story simply? Life doesn't take a straight line. We are not linear beings. In this case I picked up three threads to answer her questions: my channeling, my teaching, and my art. None of them came first – they all happened simultaneously. As a child, I was aware of 'other dimensions.' I remember walking up the hill in my neighborhood (how old could I have been, 8 or 9?), giving a friend's 5-year-old sister advice, reinforcing a feeling of confidence in my guidance or teaching. I always drew…never stopped drawing. I sometimes wonder if this is simply because no one discouraged me. I know others who stopped making art when faced with harsh judgment from teachers or professors. All three of these aspects of myself developed at once: the spirituality, the teaching, the art. Or perhaps, they were simply revealed at once. Perhaps I came into this life with each fully intact. If there was an obstacle to overcome, it was being silenced when I offered advice at the dinner table (usually my older brother being the topic of discussion). After all, I was a child, and a female child at that. What did I know?

We believe wisdom comes from experience – in the past, elders have been appreciated for their wisdom after learning life's tough lessons. I believe that wisdom comes from an inner source when we have tapped into Guidance through openness or receptivity to a higher level of consciousness. Children haven't learned yet to block out those sensory impulses, and some children – especially children who spend much time alone, remain open to it. What I did not include in my story was that at age twelve, I was put into quarantine due to infectious hepatitis and spent eight months by myself, my only contact being my mother bringing food into my room. This preceded my father's death when I was thirteen and heard him speak my name.

As a young adult, I was attracted to the subject of spirituality – all that I felt but had not been taught. We avoid this topic like the plague; it is taboo in the world of religion. I recently watched the film *Fatima*, about the ten-year-old child and her two younger friends who had visions of the Virgin Mary; no one else could see Her, but because of their religious faith, some people believed the child truly did communicate with Mary. Others cruelly harassed her, even though Mary was central to their religious practice. Anyone who claims such visions risks being called crazy at best, or fraudulent at worst. The question posed in the film was why would Mary appear to a mere child? I would answer because she hadn't unlearned the openness required.

As a busy mother, graduate student, artist, gallery owner, women's group leader, and activist, I had to find a way to manage my time; I developed what I called a house diagram – each room in the house representing a field of activity. Within that, I could write the tasks I needed to accomplish. The attic contained my goals, the basement my foundation – the values and beliefs my life was built upon. This allowed me to seek and find balance in my life: no one room took precedence. This took practice and discipline. As I write about in the book, the deeper my spiritual life became, the more I found the necessity for not just balance, but integration. I could no longer keep these various activities separate: my meditation informed my art, my art informed my teaching, and so on. Eventually, I've come to the realization that balance and integration are not enough: synthesis is called for. All aspects of who I am are operating simultaneously. This is what this book is about: the parts of the whole, their balance, their integration, and their synthesis. Although I have spoken about most of what I've written here to my two closest friends and attuned family members (there are a few), my student's questions have led me to putting it all down in one place. Is it the whole story? No. That would take a whole other lifetime to tell, and another for you to read. I've chosen some highlights and shared them here with you.

Many blessings,

Nancy Winternight

# 1

## Channeling

It all started with this book.[1] I was in the Omega Bookstore in Rhinebeck in 1992 and was attracted by the painting on its cover. In the book, the authors described what they called the *GRACE* method for learning to communicate with angels. I opened the cover, and the angels began to speak. Needless to say, I bought the book.

Here's a sampling of the simple messages I received in the beginning: *grow your hair; buy colored pencils; write down what you hear. Grow your hair,* because hair actually acts as a receptor – I learned later that Native Americans believe that their hair is an extension of their nervous system, which allows them psychic or sixth sense abilities. *Buy colored pencils* because they wanted me to channel these higher vibrational energies through my hands, which literally

---

[1] Daniel, A; Wyllie, T; Ramer, A. *Ask Your Angels.* New York, Wellspring/Ballantine, 1992.

began to vibrate as I was guided to draw what I perceived as angelic form. I kept a notebook of these drawings which were meant to attune me to a higher frequency. Here are two.

**Write down what you hear:** As I spent more time attuning, I sat in meditation and received long messages. The problem was, I couldn't remember them afterwards. Writing them down, and then typing them with my word processor, I could refer back to the messages as well as feel affirmed that this had actually taken place. I did this for some time – I could write the messages, but I didn't feel I could speak them out loud. In 1993, I traveled to a conference in Sedona, Arizona where I spent much time meditating in my motel room, communicating with higher level beings like Archangel Metatron, and also slammed my thumb badly in my rental car door, which apparently opened a creative meridian in my arm. After that, I could speak what I heard out loud.

Over the next several months, my abilities increased. I channeled Pleiadians (beings from the Pleiades) who, I came to understand from other channelers, decorated their homes with flying figures. I, myself, had been painting flying women since 1989. I communicated with a dark-haired woman called Mraoona, who dressed in a flightsuit with a triangular insignia, introducing me to the fact that there were other beings interested in the ascension of our planetary consciousness on Earth and were making themselves available to support our efforts. My channeling, offered through groups - first in my Stone Ridge art gallery and then in my Ashokan home, sometimes brought through Mother Mary, Sananda (the soul level energy of Jesus), Kwan Yin, as well as some other ascended masters, but my main source of information eventually came to be my personal angelic guides, Alandriel and Galadriel, who are associated with Archangel Michael. People could ask personal questions, the answers to which I would not have known otherwise. Participants reported that the sessions gave them a profound sense of peace.

Also in 1993, I got a call from our friend Alex, telling me that I just HAD to read a book called *Eleven, Eleven*. Trusting him implicitly, I ordered the book and upon opening the package, saw instead, glowing in metallic silver on a pure white cover, *11:11*.[2] I'd been seeing this repeatedly on my clock for quite some time – I'm not even sure how long. My reaction was, *Ahhhh!!!* In the book, Solara explained in mythological terms the planetary shift in consciousness that we were ushering in. She spoke about the Bird Tribe and the family of An. She said we'd remember our location in the bird formation (I immediate felt and saw my location in the righthand side of the bird's neck). 11:11 was an activation code to awaken our consciousness, opening a gateway to ascension. Since that time, more and more people have noticed it on their clocks. It's not something you're looking for, it just shows up. People have misinterpreted it as a sign of good fortune, but it really has to do with awakening. It sometimes shows up to reassure you that you're on the right path, in sync with the emerging paradigm. I associate the number 11 with the angels, and here it appears twice. Note the upward pointing triangle with a circle at the top on the cover. This will become significant in my discussion of the merkabah and sacred geometry.

---

[2] Solara. *11:11*. Whitefish, Star Borne, 1992.

Over the years, the channeling groups fell away as I became more involved in my college teaching and eventually with Expressive Arts. When doing units on spirituality for classes, I led guided meditations, and although I would offer the occasional personal channeling session to a client or friend, I no longer pursued it as a public endeavor. I continued my work as an artist and professor.

As a child growing up in upstate New York, I was quite aware that Indians had either once lived on our property or had walked through it…I can't explain how I knew this, just a kind of knowing, especially when I looked out a window at the back of our house. When I was thirteen, my father died. On the second day after his passing, I heard him call "Nancy" in his voice. My immediate response, out loud, was "What?" At that moment I understood that there are other dimensions - it's not just what we can see here. Time passed…my now brother-in-law gave me and my then boyfriend, now husband, a copy of Ram Dass's book *Be Here Now* [3] which resonated deeply. After that, I sought out whatever books on spirituality I could find. My very first experience of receiving information occurred in October of 1975. My husband, Robert, had an interest in intentional communities – places where people lived on communal land with shared values and ideals. He'd heard of Findhorn in northern Scotland, where we visited on a trip to the UK. Findhorn had developed out of the experiences of Dorothy

---

[3] Dass, Ram. *Be Here Now*. San Cristobal, Lama Foundation, 1971.

Maclean, Eileen Caddy, and Eileen's husband Peter. The women received information in meditation from the plant *devas* (spirits) for tending to the plants in the garden. The results were phenomenal, and a small community grew up around that garden. When we arrived there, we discovered that they were closed that day for Michaelmas, but we bought a few books at the bookstore and stayed the night nearby in the Cluny Guest House, which has since become a part of Findhorn. All night long, I heard "Beware of kings, beware of kings." The next day we drove back to England, finally arriving in Oxford. Robert mistakenly drove the wrong way down a one-way street in search of a parking space so that we could grab some lunch. He was pulled over by the police, at which time I noticed we were stopped directly in front of Kings College, on Kings Road. This was not by any means a profound channeling experience, but affirmed to me that I had this capacity to receive communication from other realms, and I've only recently learned that Findhorn's "power point" is located directly behind Cluny.

When we returned from that trip, we rented a small bungalow in the woods in the Catskills, near the infamous Woodstock, where we stayed through the winter. I'd like to share one experience I had in that house (more to come). It was a snowy day and Robert had gone out to run an errand. I was soaking in the tub when I had a powerful, palpable sense that something – or someone – was passing over the house. I don't think I've ever had a sense like that since. When Robert got home, he asked, "Did you see the snowy owl?!" Well, I hadn't seen it, but I sure had felt it! Now, 46 years later, I have painted a large canvas of the recent vision of a white owl, called *Sacred Geometry: Wisdom & Guidance*.

In April of 1976, while we were still renting that house, a devotee of the Siddha, Swami Muktananda, a *sadguru* (true guru) who traveled around spreading his teaching *God Dwells Within You As You*, placed a full page ad in the *Woodstock Times*, our local newspaper. Baba, as he was called, would be arriving in the Catskills, and we were invited to meet him. Robert and I went. Sitting in a group of other seekers, we were led in a chant: *Om Namah Shivaya* - I bow to the inner self, as we awaited Baba's arrival. Apparently, the flight from India had been delayed, so we were chanting for a *very* long time. When he eventually arrived and sat upon a thronelike seat at the front of the room, we were invited to join the darshan line, where devotees offered simple gifts of fruit or flowers to the guru as he brushed their heads and faces with peacock feathers. I didn't know you were supposed to bring a gift and felt awkward about going up in line before this great being without one! So I didn't go. That night, I had a dream. Baba came to me and offering me an orange, simply said, *I hope we'll get to know each other better.* I got out of bed, and standing in our kitchen, I ate an orange.

After that, I began a Siddha Yoga meditation practice, using the instructions Baba provided in his books and talks. In his autobiography, *Play of Consciousness*, Baba described his own process of enlightenment and his philosophy that God exists in our very being.[4] How can we not think highly of ourselves, honor ourselves, and live the fullest expression of ourselves if we are in essence God? I should also mention that Ram Dass had written the introduction to this book. In the years following, we spent much time with our beloved guru after he established his ashram in South Fallsburg, a 45-minute ride from our home. Baba had a way of making you think he was speaking just to you in his native Hindi, even if you were in a hall with hundreds of other devotees. Every word was translated by the now Gurumayi Chidvilasanda, his successor. Once, attending an intensive in which he offered *shaktipat* – the awakening of the dormant kundalini or meditation energy at the base of the spine, we were informed shortly ahead of time that we were to purchase a copy of a particular chant to the Divine Mother for the morning session. I dutifully did so. However, when it came time for the chant, it was obvious that I, in the hall of 500 people or more, was the only one who had done so. I, alone, chanted with Baba. I cannot tell you how intimate that felt as my tears flowed.

One particular experience I'd like to share here is when I decided to offer Baba a small shell, which I felt very deeply represented the simplicity of my being.

---

[4] Baba Muktananda Paramahansa. *Play of Consciousness*. California, Shree Gurudev Siddha Yoga Ashram, 1974.

Waiting for my turn in the darshan line, I consciously infused that shell with this intended message. And when it was my turn, I handed Baba the shell directly (most gifts were placed at his feet). Baba turned the shell over in his hand and examined it quite thoroughly, and then made a throaty *UHN* sound – an acknowledgment of what I had wished to communicate. Now, whenever I feel I have to do MORE - for example, sound more professional to be taken seriously or do MORE to fulfill myself, I remember the simplicity of that shell and Baba's recognition of...me. Simply to be myself is enough.

Siddha Yoga meditation enhanced my ability to sense energy. Sometime around 1978, we bought a loaf of bread at our local health food store from The Abode. I didn't know anything about The Abode, except that it was located in the general vicinity of where the Shakers had lived, not far from where I grew up in upstate New York. I remember so clearly eating the bread and sensing its high vibrational energy. I felt moved to write them a letter to say how high the bread was! Unfortunately, Robert discouraged me from mailing the letter – what kind of a kook mails a letter to a bakery to say they sensed how high their bread is? I didn't mail the letter. Later I learned that Ram Dass had established his base and was living at The Abode, a Sufi meditation center. Lesson: trust yourself. It's real.

Baba died in 1982. I'd had a dream visitation from him within a night or two beforehand, and our kitchen clocked stopped at the exact moment of his death. What Baba Muktananda gave me was the ability to attain realms in meditation, waking in the night with amber light seemingly shining behind my head, visions in meditation of the tiny seedlike blue pearl, feelings of levitation in meditation and transcendance in life, and access to bliss. He fostered my fullest creativity and self-expression.

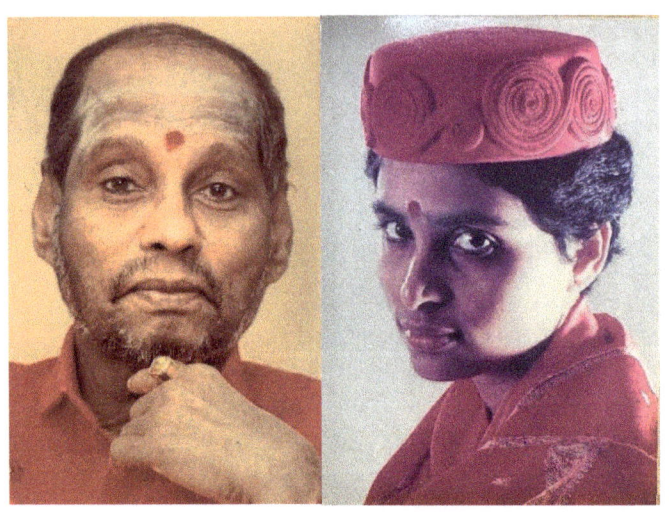

Photos: SYDA Foundation

Baba Muktananda and Gurumayi Chidvilasananda

In the fall of 1998, Robert and I purchased an old farmhouse on Cape Breton Island, Nova Scotia, where we had been visiting since we were still in college. The following summer, we were able to spend the entire summer there, the first time in the twenty-seven years we'd been going. That was the summer I had a herniated disc in my back, and needless to say, was in a great deal of pain. When we arrived that summer, we discovered that the people who owned the property two doors up from us were planning to build a house high on the hill and tear down the old Acadian farmhouse below, where the wife had grown up. Over the years, this had been one of our favorite houses – it had the Acadian truncated gable, designed to hold the roof down in the extreme winds, and the historic blue shingled roof. We had thought the year before when we purchased our house, that the old structure would make an excellent studio. So when we arrived this summer, and our neighbor informed us that the house would be destroyed, we asked if we could move it to our property. And we did. Beforehand, though, we toured the building, which was full of old furniture and relics that the the owners didn't want. I found a very old, slightly faded and partially insect-eaten picture of what appeared to be a nun holding roses, and brought her to our house, setting her on my dresser where I could have a clear view from my bed.

If you've ever had a herniated disc, then you know the pain I'm talking about. I spent much of my time on my bed, trying not to grit my teeth. Oddly, the old picture was giving me a great deal of comfort. Finally one day, I simply asked, "Who are you?" Immediately, I heard, "Therese" – not Theresa, but the French Therese. Of course, we were in the Acadian region of Cape Breton, where the residents mainly speak a French dialect, so I wasn't terribly surprised. But as someone raised Jewish, I had no knowledge whatsoever of Catholic saints. And not until I was finally able to get some information upon returning to New York, did I realize this was St. Therese of Lisieux, a Carmelite nun born in France in 1873, who only lived to be 24 and is highly regarded on Cape Breton. Eventually, I was able to read her autobiography, which she struggled to finish before her death.[5] That picture of St. Therese still sits on my dresser in Cape Breton. There are more holes in the paper, despite it being under glass. The picture is slowly disappearing, perhaps adding to the meaning of the word *holy*. But I still feel that strong connection, and Therese's autobiography is one of the few books I've kept after all these years.

---

[5] St. Therese of Lisieux. *Story of a Soul.* Washington, ICS Publications, 1996.

St. Therese of Lisieux

Robert and our daughter, Juda, left to return to the States at the end of the summer. I stayed. At the end of one week, women from my WAVE group would be coming to join me for a week-long workshop of what I called A Journey Deeper, using Expressive Arts to gain inner knowledge. I had no car and no company, only my art. That week alone felt like a very holy time for me, and I painted a series of what would become painted quilts – self-portraits in prayer. These felt very Catholic to me – in fact, I knew I'd had at least one life as a nun. I remember finishing one of these paintings, and saying out loud to myself, "I've found my nun," which was followed by an immediate knock on the door! Opening it, I found a soft-spoken, somewhat jittery, silver-haired woman who told me her grandmother had lived next door, and as a girl she had visited our house many times. This was, yes, Sister Ellen, Ellen Donovan, one of the Sisters of Charity from Glace Bay, with whom, as it turned out, I had much in common. Working as a massage therapist with the poor women of Glace Bay, she had a rather radical view of women in the Catholic church. We really hit it off. At one point, when I mentioned I was from Ashokan, she gasped that her favorite piece of music was Jay Ungar's *Ashokan Farewell,* and don't you know, I had a cassette tape of it.

As I played it for her, she sat in absolute reverie. I had indeed found my nun. Sister Ellen and I corresponded over the years by letter, and occasionally, she'd pop up at our house in the summers. She was a very dear soul, close to my heart. Who would think a nice, Jewish girl like me would make friends with a Catholic nun?

Just before that summer, before the herniated disc, I traveled (again) to the UK, this time to be a presenter at the CHARTS symposium on arts and health, in Manchester. While there, I met an extraordinary woman, June Boyce-Tillman – a British composer, professor of performing arts, head of the Hildegard Network, and now Anglican priest. I followed June to Shropshire, where she was presenting a workshop on Hildegard of Bingen, a 12th century German abbess – *a visionary, a musician, a dramatist, and an abbess*[6]. I would add to this list, healer – Hildegard believed that when we are out of harmony with Nature, we are vulnerable to illness, whether this be individually or collectively as a society. When I accompanied June to the old monastery in Ludlow where the workshop would take place, she dressed in draping maroon, I was walking behind her as she opened the door to our rooms (quite like cells), and had a memory of her as *my* abbess in a past lifetime. June's presentations (I have now seen several, including one she did in Cape Breton) as well as her book have helped me to understand who Hildegard was as a model for someone fully engaged with creativity – every aspect fully integrated and realized. Hildegard had visions of angels, and her musical compositions, which were sung by her nuns, were at such a high octave (difficult for singing), elevated to the level of the angels and tapping into the highest level of our chakra system, gave the term *choirs of angels* meaning. Thankfully, Hildegard's music has now been recorded.[7]

Early in September, 2001, I had a dream. I was standing in a tall building looking out a large window at what looked like long, mechanical arms scooping snow. Two days later, the attack on the Twin Towers took place. When I saw the images on TV the next morning, I realized that it hadn't been snow in the dream,

---

[6] Boyce-Tillman, June. *The Creative Spirit*. Harrisburg, Morehouse Publishing, 2001.
[7] Anonymous 4. Hildegard von Bingen, *11,000 Virgins.*, France, Harmonia Mundi, 1997.

but ash being scooped by large cranes. Three days after the 11th, I had a vision of thousands of angels facilitating the upward movement out of the rubble of the victims' spirits. Being able to see these kinds of visions puts events in perspective for me – a witness consciousness, with less attachment to the emotion, and greater perception of the overall picture. George Harrison died soon after, on November 29th, meaning he would have ascended three days later on my birthday. The path he had opened for so many of us through the teachings inherent in his lyrics was profound. It felt to me that this was somehow all connected, a major shift in consciousness. In fact, even for a short time after September 11th, we seemed more aware of our deep connection with each other – not just in the US, but with others around the world. It was the first wake up call.

## Grounding the Energy

I have recently been told in meditation that the UK is a portal for me, a place where I can access higher level energies, and that I go there when I'm ready for a change in my life. My younger daughter and I took a trip to the UK in the fall of 2018. Something seemed to shift for me then. I'd been painting my flying women at that point for nearly 30 years. When people asked me why the women were flying, I patiently answered it was a representation of spirit, the way I felt in my waking state - uplifted. My meditation practice had become irregular – I could still channel easily for people when asked, but after returning from that trip, I felt the directive from my guides to sit every morning for meditation.

It did not take me long to establish a routine: wake up, drink a cup of tea, sit for meditation with a quartz crystal in one hand – in fact, the one I had purchased on my trip to Sedona...twenty-five years earlier. I was quite aware of the presence of my angelic guides, associated with Archangel Michael. Holding the crystal high above my head, I tapped into quite an elevated state of consciousness. I found that my guides had their own ideas in mind. I began to receive the image of a painting I was supposed to make – a self-portrait as an angel. There were very specific instructions regarding the area around my head – I was supposed to expand the typical halo which I had often included in my paintings, to include the area of the heart with particles of light. I called this painting, *Gloria Caelesti* (Celestial Glory), the title received in meditation. After these came two more in this Winternight Trinity: *Stella Spiralus* and *Spiritus*.

Winternight Trinity: *Gloria Caelesti*, *Stella Spiralus*, and *Spiritus*

These paintings, created over the course of the next year, represented three aspects of myself: spiritual being, teacher, and artist. As a humanistic educator, I've felt my purpose is to encourage my students to become the fullest expression of who they are (informed by Baba's teachings), which entails a process of transformation – hence, the magic wand in *Stella Spiralus* (Star Spiral). The paintbrush and palette in *Spiritus* (Spirit) mimic the sword and shield of Archangel Michael. Together, the three paintings depicted who I was – who I am, really, as a multidimensional being.

What I knew at the end of the process of creating these three paintings was that I couldn't go back to my usual flying women. Allowing myself to be guided in the morning meditations, I realized that I have become a painter of energy. I was instructed to draw energetic mandalas after meditation, using oil pastels – simply sketches of what I had seen or felt during meditation. The colors varied from day to day, and a short statement usually accompanied them. Eventually, I understood that I was to start painting them – LARGE. The impulse was to paint on very large canvases, but I have a tiny studio and stressed a bit about how big they wanted me to go, and how heavy a canvas I could lift. I eventually settled on a manageable size of one square yard, light enough to lift, but large enough to encompass the energy coming through. Again, specific images and instructions were provided. This is when Archangel Metatron arrived.

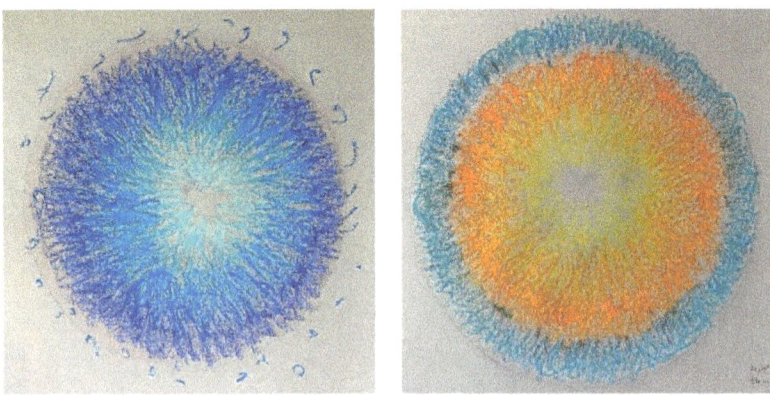

Oil pastel mandalas: images I had seen in meditation

Upon closing my eyes since the beginning of this process, I have seen a white illumination in my upper left field of vision, just outside of the mandala, not quite circular, which I associate with my angelic guides. Metatron has made himself known by a bright white disc at the very top of my vision field. The mandalas appear at the center when I'm focused on my third eye, whether or not the room is dark, and often at the top of the merkabah's front-facing triangle (see the *11:11* cover). The paintings could take weeks or more, depending on the amount of light available in my studio (boo to cloudy days and rain) and my teaching schedule. First, I was told that the three - Michael, Sananda, and Metatron were working together as a unit, and I should think of them as The Ones, rather than individual entities. It became evident through the messages that I would now be working with Sacred Geometry (Metatron's specialty). He said, *Geometry is the structure of all living matter; Sacred Geometry is the structure of consciousness.* What was I to do with this kind of information, except follow the path opening before me? It was suggested to me to explore the Kabbalah's tree of life. Without going into too much detail, I understood from which part of that structure this information was coming. I understood where I was hanging out during meditation. I saw an image of Da Vinci's Adam and understood that the structure of our bodies is tied to the energy of the tree of life. I read about the prophet Ezekiel's vision of the merkabah, which was what I was seeing in my meditation. Painting after painting, the images shifted in color and pattern, but all are what I call color wheels or *energy mandalas,* depicting the energy of the Universe, emanating from one central point of light.

These paintings are a way to ground the new higher dimensional energies pouring forth to our planet during this time of transformation. It is essential to put the energies into form. Each of us has a way of our own to do that – it might be through gardening, or making music, or building new forms of architecture. It might be redesigning the spaces we live in to incorporate more of who we are becoming. For me, it is through the painting. My hope is that people who view them will feel that within themselves as well.

Left: *Sacred Geometry, Intuition*   Right: *Sacred Geometry: Shakti*

I was told: *the energy at the top of the merkabah is activating*, and was provided with an activation code to access it. The merkabah, two interlinking tetrahedrons – one facing upwards and one down, is used to travel to other dimensions. Now, when I enter meditation, I travel upwards. Whenever I'm working on an image and am struggling with how to bring the energy into form (how do you paint light and energy?), the image is right there for me, with a simple explanation. If I question how to paint it, I hear, *We can provide an image to the artist, but it's the artist who brings it into form*. This gives me some free reign in the interpretation.

Whenever my heart center has been engaged in the energetics, Sananda has come through with messages for me. I was told,

*The heart has wings; the wings are invaluable to the evolution of Oneness.*

*The wings are an expansion of the heart. Opening the wings, opens the heart.*

I believe at this time, we are being called upon to see our interconnection with others. Once we become aware of our shared human experiences, we open to others – we see more unity and less division. When others suffer, our hearts open with compassion; we understand we are not alone in this life, but instead are all in this together. If you think about the location of the heart chakra in the middle of the chest and where wings would be attached if we had them, you can see that it's the same place in the body. The winged heart is a symbol in Sufism (you see how there is a interlacing of experience? – Ram Dass was living at The Abode, a Sufi center). And here I am receiving messages about the heart and wings. The wisdom is universal. Sananda also said:

*Do not think of yourself as separate; you are a part of a divine network.*

This simply reinforces the idea that we are not alone. Each one of us is an essential piece of the Whole – essential because without each and every one of us, the Whole is incomplete. When I support my students to become their fullest selves, it is so that we can complete the picture – each and every one of us, the fullest expression of who we are, each with a unique purpose. As Muktananda taught us: *God Dwells Within You as You* – be that full expression. An aspect of this to understand is that when we deny others full participation, whether that be through racism or any other form of oppression, we cheat ourselves of their fullest contribution to the Whole. This is why *Black Lives Matters* and other movements to end oppression against marginalized groups are crucial now. This world needs everyone.

Other messages have come through in the way of simple teachings, very often presented in doublets:

*The sequence of events allows the illusion of time within the paradigm.*
*But beyond the paradigm, is only timelessness – all is eternal.*

Time has appeared linear in the old paradigm due to the perception of one experience happening after another. But beyond the paradigm(s), is only timelessness (the eternal). That's why, when we make a practice of tapping into the deep inner self in meditation, we are not thrown about by external events, but remain rooted in the experience of that steady, eternal part of ourselves.

As I write this, we are shifting from one dimension to another and starting to operate at a higher frequency. While we're in this process of change from one to the other, there will be a pulsating effect, back and forth...so sometimes the day seems right, and on another the day feels off – thinking that Friday is Saturday or Monday is Sunday. Because we are beginning to operate at a higher level of consciousness, there will be more experiences of things happening at the same time – less linear. I tell friends who struggle with this confusion about time to make a mind map – to see the branches of one's experiences all at once.

*The purpose of the Self is to see one's place in the Infinite.*
*The purpose of the All is Oneness.*

To me, this is the key teaching coming through right now. Yes, we are individuals. When we see our interconnecting values as pieces of the Whole, there is that sense of Oneness. I am That That I am – I am That Higher Consciousness. In fact, we are all That. Soon after George Harrison died in 2001, this came through in its entirety. All it needs is a bit of slide guitar.

### *Lightness of Being*

Channeled by George Harrison

May it come to pass
That my heart embraces
The spirit of being
My Lightness of Being.

Though life may pull me
The world will twirl me
The spirit of seeing
My Lightness of Being
Brings me back
To the One inside me.

That I may know you
That I may show you
The Lightness of Being
One with You.

## How to attune to angels

The authors of *Ask Your Angels* described a key process of learning to communicate with angels, using the word GRACE to represent the progressive steps, standing for *grounding, releasing, aligning, communicating,* and *enjoying.* The following explanations are my own.

**Grounding** is important. We are energy receptors, receiving impulses all the time – from each other, from the natural and unnatural worlds around us, and even from other realms whether we're aware of it or not. Being grounded allows that electrical flow upwards and downwards, as the energy passes through our system, through the *shushumna* surrounding the spine. Not being grounded would mean we could not embody this sometimes intense energy; being grounded helps to support it. In terms of the chakra system, when our root chakra is connected to the Earth, we feel stable, balanced and secure. Receiving any energy without that grounding means we are unable to easily return to the physical body – we certainly wouldn't want to experience being 'lost in space.' I've been told that it's essential to embody the new energies pouring into our world. We are instructed to *ground* it, to put it into form. It's imperative to be grounded ourselves to do so.

*You are the embodiment of this energy. Incorporate this light into the physicality of your being. Live as lightly as you can.*

How do we ground? Being in nature helps – taking a walk, gardening, hugging a tree, or doing simple domestic tasks like washing dishes (it helps if you have a window to look outdoors). *Earthing* is a term for walking outdoors barefoot to connect with energies emanating from the ground. In meditation, we can imagine sending roots down into the Earth from our root chakra, or feet if we are sitting in a chair. By anchoring ourselves in Earth energy, we can experience that grounding, offering ourselves a solid base from which to proceed.

**Releasing** is easier for some than others. We want to let go of anything holding us back from progressing on our spiritual path. This might be former experiences or beliefs which do not allow us to accept that we can be open to receive a higher level energy. Some of these beliefs may be about not feeling good enough or being limited in our abilities, or fear of moving into the unknown. We need to let go of doubt, and trust in our capacity. The more we can release, the more space becomes available to us to create what's new in our lives, to become more of ourselves, and in this case, more open to receiving communication. I've found using expressive arts to be very helpful – using clay, drawing or painting, making sound, or creative movement, without preconception, as means to clear out old patterns and open to what's possible. In meditation, we can imagine letting go of tension or what no longer serves us as we outbreathe. You can even imagine sending that old energy down the roots into the Earth – don't worry, the energy will be recycled, just as compost becomes nourishment for your garden.

**Aligning** is the key component of the process of readying yourself to communicate with angels. Anything that promotes centering is helpful. What helps you to center? To feel your core self? Some students of mine report this when completely absorbed in doing expressive arts. I sense it when painting. Most effective, I think, is practicing chakra meditation. When each energy center is open and aligned, we have keen capacity for receiving energy. By simply attuning to each chakra in meditaton, we can achieve this sense of centering and alignment. The guided white light meditations I offer give participants that direct experience. And, for example, an exercise of welcoming your Guide into your heart during meditation and asking a question, can surprise you with the ease of reception. Trust that what you hear is true. Write it down immediately, so that you don't forget.

I believe that a regular, disciplined, practice of meditation is the most effective means of establishing the receptivity you need for communication: meditating at the same time each day, sitting in the same spot which you only use for meditation; wearing the same clothes or a particular shawl; and tapping into the space between the breaths – the entry point to the inner self. As you breathe, notice where the inbreath meets the outbreath. If your attention wanders, simply bring it back to the breath. The more absorbed you are in the inner self, the greater your inner focus, and the more sensitive you become to these transmissions. A mantra can also help to hold your attention as you learn to become absorbed. Eventually, it becomes second nature.

**Communicating:** ask and you shall receive. As a young artist, I decided I needed a name. Not my birth name, which I did not relate to (it had been changed three generations back), and not my married name – my husband was also an artist, and I didn't want to be signing the same name to my work. I sat for meditation and stated out loud, "I need a name." This was a strong and clear intention of receiving something, though I had no idea what. After a few minutes, I experienced a rising, 'bubbling up' sensation – bloop, bloop, bloop, bloop, bloop: *Winternight*. I really didn't know what to make of this, but if you were to see my art at that time (woven tapestries), it often included images of crescent moons and stars. Honestly, the name made sense. I was hesitant at first to use it, but grew into it. I began signing my work Winternight, and now my students address me as Professor Winternight.

All we need to do is ask. What is it you want to know? What do you want to receive? Ask. Then remain receptive in meditation – just be open. See what comes through.

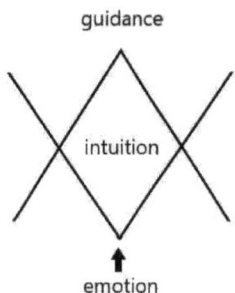

One teaching to come through during my morning meditations was the statement, *Guidance from Above mixes with the emotions of physicality to create intuition.* I was shown the two v's – one open at the top, the other below, overlapping each other, much like the merkabah's six-pointed star comprised of the overlapping triangles, one directed upwards towards the heavens, the other downwards towards Earth. The only difference here was that the triangles remained open. The upper v directed guidance downward toward the center, the lower v directed emotion located in the body upwards toward the center. The meeting of the two, I was told, creates our ability to feel or understand through our intuitive knowing. To me, this is another reason to engage in expressive arts, which allow us to feel emotion. Combining this with the higher level guidance from our guides (let's face it, they're trying to get through to us all the time, if only we'd pay attention), develops this ability. We've got our own inner guidance system, if we attune to it.

For me, it's extremely helpful to sit in my morning meditation sessions and simply tune into guidance. Each session ends with a 'private reading' – a message that helps me to know how to spend my day, what my next steps are, what to expect in the future. I may feel angels working on me to heal areas of my body in need of attention, or receive instructions for specific exercises to help with a physical issue. If I'm sore or unwell, I may hear *you'll feel better by Tuesday*, and then when Tuesday arrives, I notice I feel better. I believe each and every one of us has this capacity if we develop it. Of course, it requires clear intention, practice, and trust in ourselves. I hope you will learn to find your own inner guidance – it's within all of us. The angels will be thrilled that you'll finally hear what they have to say!

Photo credit: Juda Leah     Brighton UK

# 2

## George, The Grandmothers, and the Angels

I recently discovered a few small notebooks, one with handwritten channeled entries from the fall of 2003 and New Year's Day, 2005. In it, was a series of messages from George Harrison, who had begun to come through daily. At some point in October of 2003, I'd flown to Florida to take my mother to the neurologist, since she'd shown growing evidence of dementia. He diagnosed her with Alzheimer's. Needless to say, her care from 1500 miles away became all-consuming. I was unable to maintain the connection with George and eventually forgot about the extent of it. My mother passed away in 2018, which indicates the length of time I was responsible for her care, though eventually we had moved her north, much closer to where I lived. Although I continued to channel on occasion, it wasn't until my trip to the UK in that year and the subsequent regularity of my daily meditation that I was able to return to my practices in full. I am happy to have rediscovered this earlier contact. George says in his last message that time is experienced differently on 'the other side' and nothing is lost. I now pick up the responsibility he gifted me at that time.

Also included in this time/channeling are communications from the Circle Spirits of the 13 Indigenous Grandmothers – the thirteen grandmothers initially met in a location very near my house, and I was able to be in attendance for the entire week-long program. Later, some others who had been in attendance helped my friend Cassia and me to organize a program to share the information about the grandmothers' message to the public in Woodstock, NY.

Finally, included are two messages from my personal angelic Guides, who have loyally worked with me for many years. To them, I am eternally grateful.

## George Harrison

**Namaste!** I am with you. Hari Krishna, Hari Bol. It is a delightful experience to be outside/without the body – there is a lightness of air which is indescribable. Take care, beware of darkness – is this not what I sang, what I warned all of you, and yet I see from here, as I saw from there that this is what is taking place – ALL of you, forgetting just why you are there – and that, in fact, we are HERE! Go within, repeat your mantra, know that God is within you (and without you). Know that Peace is what you make it. If you desire it, then you must create it. If I were THERE I would sing these words, write these songs, but I am no longer in body, but I am spirit and from HERE, the messages must be received by others – those of you who heard them before – those of you who were with me before, as you were, as you know and remember. (Seven pools). And so, dear ones, those of you who are heart-connected, never fear, for God is All That Is, and "His" fullest expression will appear in all His Glory. Know that by seeking Peace within and expressing Peace without YOU ARE FULFILLING OUR DESTINY. It's really very simple.

And so we will meet, you and I, every day at this time (when you can) and Please Know that all that happens from here on is meant to lead you where you need to be so that your energies will be used to the Greatest Good. Enjoy! Hari Bol!

I am G. Harrison
Servant of Krishna
This day 9/10/03


**Hari Bol, Hari Bol**, so good to be with you again today! From this perspective I can see the world from a broader view – people running willy nilly about the place like worker ants. Where's the sense of higher purpose? Where's the sense of devotion to God? From here we see those of you who desire a different outcome. Careful. Beware of darkness! Know that you are creating the new world. Adhere to the

new light pouring into your atmosphere for it holds the key, that unlocks the heart to a New Way of Being. Take care, beware you are here to live differently! Please know this is true. My heart connects with those who recognize the true reason for being here, and in the coming weeks I hope to send light into your heart and mind for you to deliver in your own peaceful way. WEAR A SHIELD for there are others who would try to inflict pain. Be a warrior of light. Be the Blue One who holds the world in (his) hand. Be the holder of light on earth. Never be afraid of revealing your light. Not everyone will heed the call, but Reveal the Truth for now is the Time. Though I am no longer in the body, my spirit is intact – in many ways it is easier to get the message out from here – for there are those of you who are willing to listen, willing to dispel the truth through your contact with others. Why else be there? Why else be anywhere? Ah, more songs to be written, more truth to be spoken – we are rich in each other, so never doubt the Truth. Go in peace, enjoy your day.
I am Geo Harrison as you knew me, know me now. ॐ
9/11/03


**It is indeed a new day**, and we can celebrate that together, whether we are in body or not. For me, being out of the material world is like a blessing – is a blessing – I never could stand the body's limitations. Now I free float, can go where I need to go unhindered. It's good to be reunited with John, too, and to find the places we connected before even more In Tune. You'll hear some of our music coming your way before long, and you'll recognize it, guaranteed.

And now for the Daily Message, as it were, as it is, as it will be, for you know that Time is only one, not split in fragments as it seems in the earth plane. Go within as often as you can – it's easy, as you know to get caught up in the daily grind. Instead, see if you can set aside moments and indeed, find moments even within the work, when you can reconnect with the Cosmos because that's why you're here – to stay in touch, reconnect higher planes of consciousness to your "ordinary" world, though deep down there's nothing ordinary about it, only Maya's veil which conceals its true nature. Find times when you bring your awareness of the Truth into your everyday waking life and then make others aware as well. Circles of awareness will grow from this – people gathering in awareness, in consciousness. John preceded me in attaining this state because he already had transcended the mundane – or a better way of saying it would be that he saw the divine – the love – in the mundane. I hung on a bit longer because I didn't trust that the message had been received, but I see now that it was, because there are layers of awareness, layers of consciousness, and the message had to be relayed to the top layer, who in turn will/have passed in on and so on. You, my beloveds, have heard me and have lived and shared this knowledge, of Our Greatness, our Divinity. You read recently Mother Teresa's words and they are true – God does not ask of us to be successful, only faithful. God will handle the rest. So go in peace, enjoy the day, celebrate the Unity of All Consciousness and remember to love, love, love…

I am, your servant, Geo. Harrison
9/13/03


**Communication comes rapidly** and easily in these times. Hari Bol to you and yours! It is exciting to be able to be with you, communicate with you in this way. Know that this *is* a time of tremendous change – you are seeing this in those around you who are no longer able or willing to hold onto what/who they used to be and are coming to a new understanding of themselves. Is this not so? And so our communication will help to verify and even solidify what is shall we say 'going down' now – literally, because what is happening now is a result of the grounding of these higher level heavenly energies. It's exciting to me because it's what I sang about All Those Years Ago and now I'm able to watch it unfold around you and around others I am in touch with.

You think of Hawaii for a moment, don't you? There will be a time when you go there, you'll see – but it is important to know that I lived there primarily to hook into these new energies which, like times of old, are descending to earth In that Place. Your friend lives there in order to be a conduit for it – you yourself go northeast for the same purpose. There are others acting as anchors in other locations as well. I'd say NEVER FEAR to be who you are. Your divine nature shows through to those who meet you – you will be sought out for this purpose, because people will recognize their need to be in touch with divinity – you will spark that awareness within themselves. Go ahead and Be Divine, humbly, and remember our time together – it was to Birth these New Energies.

Hari Bol – a year, a month, a day, a moment, a breath of delight to you. All is well, in kindness I am Geo. Harrison on this day
9/15/03 ॐ


**Listen, take care, beware** of soft shoe shufflers, who take you where you do not go. Good morning to you – happy to be here again! You see a clear path ahead, don't forget to take the time to relax and be – find the place within that calls to you – resonates with you and gives you peace.

It seems to me as though there is a great deal of deception going on these days – you can see beyond it – people willing to believe what their leaders say, rather than believing in, trusting in their own hearts. **That's** where the shift must take place – people taking into their own hearts what's real or not. When there is such suffering in the world, you know people are looking to others to solve their fears, to solve their problems. Only you can know your own truth and act on it – live from the place of inner knowledge and bliss.

> Sat    chit    ananda

These ought to be banner words that all life is lived from – EXISTENCE, AWARENESS (KNOWLEDGE), BLISS.

You are, you have reflective self-awareness,
Your state is bliss.

Such is the nature of Truth, and nothing more. Such holy words to live by. You can spend some time contemplating this Truth and then pass it onto others.

Existence – we **are**. I **am**. Simple self-acceptance. Knowledge. I see and know myself. I know my truth. And **bliss** – our very nature, within us. Everyone's so busy looking for it elsewhere, but it's right here, right now.

You know it's true
I'm coming back to you
Never leave you behind
Your heart for humankind.
And so we speak, we laugh, we sing
And to this end, peace we'll bring!
You see? Nothing's lost, nothing's gained
And to this end, peace will reign.

Go in peace, enjoy your day!
Bliss is yours
I am, in service, G. Harrison
9/17/03

**A note**: 9/18
I chose to run errands a day early due to impending tropical storm Isabella. Walking through Filene's shortly after 10:00, I hear George Harrison singing over the loudspeaker, *I've got my mind set on you…*

**Congratulations on being here** at the right time this morning! Yes, we can arrange many things from this side – it is like play for us here. You have an advantage in that you can physically manipulate objects, but here it is done though focus – that is the only word I can use to describe the process. Anyway, I am happy to have you back today so that we can continue our "dialogue," yes, I know I am the one doing the talking here, but if at any time you have a question, simply pose it.

You ask why you are in 'tune,' listening to my endless sermons, yes! Well, you and I have a long history - not just in this life, but in lives prior. You know that we were together in Ireland as priest and nun, or what would have been the equivalent, and there were other times as well, always in a religious/spiritual context. In this life – in your life, that is, there is a need, a desire, to continue the spiritual work we began long, long ago, and that is to bring an understanding to the world of things unseen, of that which drives the Universe, but is not observed. There is a palpable energy throbbing through the fabric of existence which you perceive, but many or most do not. It is that energy – that divine bliss – that "greening power," that love which must be illumined I ask, we who work together here in this cause ask, that you continue to jot/receive this information for us and incorporate it into the work that you do. All done in modesty – for that was the drawback in my existence, my physical existence, that notoriety – though it allowed me to get my message through (at times), the fame disallowed me from active participation in disseminating it actively. You have the ability to distribute the information via your work with others – which will continue to grow. You will be able to tell people to stop running around with their heads cut off and TUNE INTO THE EVERLASTING THROB/PULSE OF LIFE. Detaching from the world, mundane by its very nature, is not an easy task and yet if we don't release its bonds on us, we live life with constrictions, never happy or at ease with ourselves, but it is not necessary to live at its mercy. This is MAYA, this is unreality, this is a shadow of what true reality holds. If **you** can disengage from it WHILE WALKING WITHIN IT, then you can achieve sainthood, you achieve what masters have sought for eternity – you attain Christ(illegible), you become that Higher Level Being you were meant to become. And so we encourage you to live in that Spirit – modestly, without the outer trappings, encumbrance of notoriety, because this actually allows you to move freely and present this work. And so I picture you in robes – which you wear ethereally, moving through the material earth plane as one among many. Simply tell people there is more than their daily grind, more than they would choose for themselves materially – more than we can even imagine – You will find a way to integrate this information in all that you do, through all that you are. You will find that people seek you out – they know on some deep inner plane that you have this knowledge, this key which will unlock their own bliss. Remember, sat chit ananda. And live by its truth. You are always existence, knowledge, bliss.

In love, light, truth, ॐ

G. Harrison, your partner this day
9/19/03

**Challenges will come your way** – it is part of the karmic aspect of life – allow these incidents to wash over you like a wave and do not cling to the distress. The sea moves inward and outward and so does the energy of life – as one thing moves in, it then recedes until the next wave of bliss. And so these are then the "backside" of the wave, the ebbing of the tide. Allow these things to melt away, to dissipate and you will notice the blissfulness of the coming of Eternity.

It is distracting for you not to have the peace and quiet necessary for focus, and yet, unless you live on a mountaintop, isolated from the world, how will you ever gain permanent blissfulness in the world? And that is to remain focused on what is real, what is true, not on the shadow or backside of the wave. Remain fixed or focused on the Godhead, and you will attain lasting eternity of Oneness with All. It is NOT necessary to practice typical meditation in that sense, but only to remain mindful of Reality, true Reality and Truth. Do you understand?

Yes.

Then I would say to you that you have grasped the message of the day – remember that you will ALWAYS draw to you the experiences necessary for you to realize this Truth, and so each "incident" is yet a reminder to Re-focus, Re-attune yourself to Spiritual Reality, to Oneness, to Light, to Devotion, to God.

All is well, enjoy this special time, and remain fixed in this Awareness of Truth.

G. Harrison
9/20/03


**We take up again today the idea of recreating our reality** – this is not new – you have been engaged in this persona for some time now – perhaps eons of time, but NOW we are faced with a crisis in the time of earth's evolution and must guide people toward stopping this destructive course of disregarding the earth's resources, its inhabitants, its air, its water, its atmosphere (in terms of emotions) because it is time for a new beginning. Those of you who are fixed in the new will appreciate that unless mass consciousness changes or shifts, catastrophic events can and will take place (like your 9-11) in order to bring people back to the awareness of spirit and away from what seems an endless fixation on the material gain and physical pleasure – material blessings and physical desire have their place – you are in fact in the body, but we have a higher purpose to serve and must not only (be aware) how to see beyond this limited view, limited perspective, but also how to integrate this higher level consciousness into daily routine so that the being here – the day-to-day activities no longer are experienced as mundane, but seem like worship, like praise, like devotion, like dance, like spiritual practice, which has its element of supreme pleasure – beyond what can only be experienced with the body's limited senses. And so how do we begin? Simply by living life from that "standpoint" and serving as a beacon of light for others to follow. Part of this will be allowing certain undersides of the wave to recede into the ocean of existence and remember the return of the crest of the wave that glimmers in the sunlight. There is balance in all things, but we dwell on wholeness and on light, and not disregarding shadow, we understand its purpose (to guide us toward the light) and hold great patience and great compassion and tolerance for those who seem to prefer the depths of the sea (so to speak).

Give God gratitude for all you do have – celebrate each and every day by bringing spirit into so-called mundane activities and know that by transforming your own life, you are transforming the world.

I am, in service, G. Harrison
9/24/03

**Good morning** – I am here with you now. You may begin to write.

YOU ARE ONE IN A MILLION. That's the beginning of a song I'm working on. I'll let you know how it develops. I'm finding more time now to devote to my music. It's funny, really, but the soul really does continue on with all its likes and dislikes, so the music will stick with me throughout the eons. I've decided to stick around here for a while until I'm needed (again) on the other side.

So this morning, let's discuss creativity and all that entails. It's a big topic, and one we tend to ignore on the other side. But really, it's at the heart of all we do, isn't it? Because we're creating all the time. *Driving down the street, our minds full of thoughts. No matter where you're focused, you'll find yourself aloft (another verse). Go with the flow.* But really whatever you're thinking IS created. That's the amazing thing. Sometimes we cancel out a thought with another. You're thinking about doing something with your life, and then along comes a thought; well, no, I can't do it, for whatever reason, and then you've cancelled it out. And you wonder why it doesn't manifest. So the idea is basically to stay out of your own way. Think the thought, speak it out loud, or write it down – then you are the Creator, not the Destroyer of your dreams. Controlling your thoughts is key to the process of creation – that's why we're such agog at the Creator's ability – look around, isn't it amazing? He didn't negate his thoughts – he kept it positive.

So have your conscious intention, but let it go and hear the Universe give you a positive response. Then step out of the way. No secret. Just discipline, really. It's why the masters chanted, to keep their focus on the Ultimate Positive, you know?

So have a great day. Enjoy, enjoy, enjoy, celebrate your own spirit and the spirits of those around you.

Sing your song, so to speak.
I am, in service, Geo Harrison
9/25/03

**The problem in the world today** is that people are turned outside in or inside out – the focus is on what's outside – what other people will think, what one Should do as opposed to the heartfelt desire within. Oh if only people searched their hearts and found the Inner Truth, but sages have been teaching this for years, and still nobody listens, nobody hears – this was my true sadness when I was in the body – we have the Sat Chit Ananda awareness, the awareness of God, and then we try to spread the word, but nobody listens. They're so caught up in their own dramas, their own soap operas – and then telling and retelling the story, or not telling at all. All we – you and I – can do is what we've done before. Continue to live our truths and speak when we have the opportunity. There's nothing else. JUST BEING HERE is enough. Let go of the notion, the idea, that you have to change Anything – it's all perfect anyway. Do your dance, sing your song, live your life – JUST BEING HERE affects the planet, affects the earth and all beings. There is so much Greatness despite the pain. There is so much Joy despite the heartache. Remember that and do the work you're here to do with gratitude. Life in the body has its limitations, but it also has its rewards and to that we say thanks.

This is a day of relief, of releasing the old shell, and making way for the new. Embrace that with all your Being – with all your beingness.

I am, in service, G. Harrison
9/26/03


**Good morning!** Let's get started. Was there anything you wanted to ask me?

Well, I could ask what the purpose of these communications is.

Yes, understandably so. You are concerned about whether others will consider these channelings legitimate, and I can understand that, especially considering my notoriety – didn't I say it always got in the way of getting the message through? Listen, it's for that very reason that I'm passing it on to you, and a few like you, who are receptive AND not only that, but aligned with the work – wanting to get the message out that it's not just this material world, but that there's so much beyond it. This material world is a mere shadow of what's real – and I've talked about that. So that's why I'm "contacting" you – to continue the message.

The message has been passed on and passed on over 1000's of years just in this way. Don't think that leaders just come up with it on their own – it's been "received" just like you're doing now. Some have revealed their source(s), some haven't. What you do with this information is up to you – it would make a nice book, wouldn't it? But it's not necessary. Give it time to become a regular part of your life and see where it goes from there. Don't worry that it will suddenly go away even if you take a short break from it – it will return if you are receptive to it. See how fast you responded to the first invitation?

So, don't fear, keep the "channels" open – and just know that it's as real as it needs to be – if it's real to you, that's enough.

So, as usual, I'm happy to be here with you. I know you've got plans for the day – I hope I can share them with you. As you work here in your studio, let the music flow...

There are other ways to stay "in tune."
Best for the day.
I am, in service to Krishna,
Geo. Harrison
9/27/03

**Time will tell** whether humanity can make this shift easily or whether it's going to take something catastrophic to wake them up. Even for you it's hard to remember why you're Here, right? So imagine someone who hasn't got a clue! Take it a day at a time – no, an hour, a minute, a second at a time and realize that NOW you have the opportunity to do what's right, what's right for the highest good of the planet, for God, for the All. At least you can do that, and sometimes that's what it will require; there's a lot of Turmoil now and it's hard to avoid being bombarded by it. So do the best you can and know that it's all unfolding as it should – be patient with yourself, feel yourself embraced by Krisna or whoever you feel most aligned with, tuned into, so to speak. There's no one way – all paths lead to God, create your own, bring the world along, all is One, you know.

So this is a dark day, in more ways than one – certain news will be revealed that will shock a few, wake up a few others – the lack of light is symptomatic of the darkness being imposed on the people of the world by the Powers of Darkness – your leadership included. Not until they choose Peace will the weather shift – people don't realize the connection.

Do what you will, stay mindful of God. All is as it needs to be.
In peace, I am, servant to Krishna, G. Harrison
9/28/03


**You have arrived!** Happy to see you again. These are incredible times, are they not? So much strife going on, so much despair set loose into the atmosphere, but also so much good intention – remember, there's ALWAYS a balance between light and dark, and so as you have more people freaked out by their lives, so you have those whose job it is to release light to counteract it. Seems like there's more work for you to do because of it – more lightgiving work than normal.

So never fear that what you're doing isn't necessary – it's actually very necessary, essential – a matter of life or death, really because everything is at stake when the balance is thrown out of balance and darkness wins. Think of Krsna and the dragon, you know – the great terrible beast he had to fight. It's not always as drastic as that – instead of one Great Being fighting the Darkness, there are a great number of you contributing your efforts for the Greater Good, the sum total of your efforts will slay the beast – in this case the negativity that has consumed the vital energy of the planet, wreaking havoc, stealing lives, laying waste…it's all a crime, a damn shame to see it, and it saddens my heart – always did, and I suppose always will. Still, there's hope! You can envision, you can imagine what Peace on earth would look like, and therefore you've got to redouble your efforts of bringing through the light.

*Light will overcome darkness.*
*Joy will overcome fear.*
*Liberation shall defeat bondage.*
*All will be free*
*All will be God*

*All is God*
*(never forget that)*
*Together we'll be One*
*We are One.*

And so, enjoy the day! It's more important than ever.

I am, in service to Lord Krsna
G. Harrison
9/29/03


**Continuing this morning** in the direction of the effort to anchor light – you see the distress all around you – you yourself express it, release it – don't hold onto it, let it pass on to those who transmute it, change it into more useful energy. It's the holding on, the aiming at others that causes the distress – whatever you send to others comes back to you a thousand-fold – why else do you think you are all as a nation experiencing what you are? If you were to send good will, kindness, humanity and love, do you think you'd be in such a state of distress?   Sing the songs that generate happiness – sing these into the atmosphere and see then what happens. Bring the tunes of consciousness to light – why do you think that chanting the names of the Lord is so powerful – for that sweetness is what comes back to you a thousand-fold. Steep yourself in bliss and then see how easy it is to wage war – it becomes impossible. Oh how we wish we could get the message through- that the true meaning of peace IS living peace – is being at peace with oneself, being at peace with the Universe, the ALL. God Bless Everyone – all the creatures great and small. **This** is the message of peace.

*Rejoice in the knowledge that this is true. Peace within is right next to you. Don't delay, I've got to say, that peace really could come today. Singing songs of peace, singing songs of joy, singing songs of bliss – it's only this, only this.*

And so enjoy your day, Winternight! Establish your own peace within and see how it spreads!

I am, in service,
G. Harrison
10/1/03

**There are often disturbances in one's life**, but again, we've got to look at water – we can think about the sea. Storms come – part of living on earth, right? But storms also pass away. So you might experience some turbulence now and again – it might even get exciting if you allow yourself the luxury of staying positive. Waves get kicked up, the bottom of the sea gets turned up and all sorts of sea animals and shells get washed ashore – maybe even stranded on the beach. But the storm passes by and everything appears normal for a while till the next storm arrives. Don't think of these special circumstances as out of the ordinary – they're part of the flow of life, the swing of emotions (don't forget emotions are very much tied to water). So when these "unusual" circumstances occur, they are just part of the flow of life – sometimes calm, sometimes stormy, sometimes in between. It doesn't make them negative or even avoidable – it's all part of the whole – you understand. It's important to have the right perspective about it, so it doesn't eat up your life force, your Shakti.

So experience Everything in the fullness of **being** (existence), even this, use it to make a whole person of yourself, a competent person – you are, you fly among the stars – always wishing for more, but understanding that you're adored – you are adored.

And so I send these wishes to you

*That all the good comes back to you*
*Never fear, staying clear*
*Of all that drags you down.*
*In love with you.*

I am in service to you
I am
G. Harrison
10/2/03


*Never going back now*
*Only forward*
*In your dreams partake*
*For our own lives we make*
*And knowing this you move toward*
*The light*

G.H.

**Together again!** It's a day to celebrate, well every day is. To celebrate our beingness, our joy in being a part of the whole, to celebrate being, an expression of the Oneness of All. Everyone "down" there forgets the celebration – they save it up for special events, when each and every moment is worth honoring, celebrating. Don't forget to capture the moments of bliss as they spin and wind around you – don't forget the atmosphere is full of light-filled particles, don't forget the consciousness that surrounds you, the love that fills you, that encompasses you. Take a moment – take them all, and celebrate.


*Stop judging and let it flow from within you.*
*Remember to say the things that fill you*
*So that all the world can hear you.*
*Repeat the words that play within you*

*And sing the praise of all that delights you.*
*These are songs of joy*
*These are songs of peace*
*And now you've created*
*What you know the world needs.*

*Sing peace*
*Sing joy*
*Sing harmony*
*Sing love*
*Sing light*
*Sing*
*Let all surround you.*

*These are works in progress*
*As we all are!*

In love Geo. Harrison
10/3/03


**Coming into play**
Playfulness in life, even in life's most distressing moments is essential in understanding that it's all a drama – it's all a play of consciousness – there is no part of life that isn't play. You teach about play (hey) and how it reduces stress, helps integrate life experience and so on, but really, play keeps you in the moment, keeps things light. An attitude of play is really helpful in keeping you sane in an insane world (and it is insane). So adopt an attitude of play – this is all an acting out of karmic reality – it's play at its core – no use fretting about it, no sense trying to avoid it – this is Reality in a very unreal way. It's the play of Maya where everyone's wearing a mask and playing a role. Keep it clear, know what the deal is – there's nothing too serious, keep it light. Laugh a bit (laugh a lot) and serve it up to God. Ask the angels to come along for the ride. It's all in fun (even the worst of it). So go in peace and enjoy the day –

*You'll take care of the tasks as they come up,*
*But keep light in your mind and heart.*
*It's a good way to start*
*Keep Maya at arm's length*
*And Krsna here in the heart.*

Om tat sat
Om tat sat
Om tat sat

I am, servant to Lord Krsna, G. Harrison
10/4/03


**Good Yom Tov (yuntuf)!** (Note: it is Yom Kippur) You see I know many languages and many ways to speak – it comes with the territory – here there is a universal language – thought form. You say it's a time to reflect but not more than any other time – if people made every day a cause to reflect, we wouldn't be in the mess we're in. Go about your business mindfully and you will receive the same benefits (maybe more) than someone else would. Otherwise you could sit for a few minutes, but it's all the same – just like we're all the same – all paths lead to God, all experience leads to God, no one is better than another. Go about your day with gratitude and grace shall descend upon you – know that the light in your heart is a beacon for all the world.

Go in peace, child, and
Enjoy the day
Geo Harrison

10/6/03

**You can hear my voice** – well, you haven't been 'here' in some time now, have you? Life will pull you in different directions and that's okay. When you're ready you'll return – you're here today. Sometimes it's necessary to relax or let go of rigid standards... Go with the flow when you remember, it's good enough. Remembering is half the battle. Being mindful is the key. Showing up is everything.

So today I wanted to talk about the key to inhabiting the body, because it's not all that easy. Most people just go along day to day – and that seems easy enough, till they end up medicating themselves for the pain – whether it's pain in the mind, or pain in the body (it's all the same distress). So it's really not so easy, that is, till you lock/look into the divine nature of things. Suddenly, it's as if you find the key to unlock the door, and it's all about remembering that you **are** divine, you **are** holy, you are God. When you haven't got the key, it's nearly impossible to get through the door of knowledge or awareness – you can try to squeeze **under** the door, you can even try penetrating the door with consciousness, but even there you're acknowledging that there's more than meets the eye. Really, the fastest, safest way through the door is unlocking it and opening it wide so you can get through pretty easily. The difficulty is in locating the key – and it'll hide itself – it's the nature of God to conceal Himself, the nature of consciousness to reveal itself, so if you look in the right place (the heart) and you're patient (trust, faith) then it's bound to show up – then, "magically" the door opens and you can see through to the other side. That's the bliss of it, moving through the door and **feeling** what's on the other side. So the work is looking in the heart, or remembering to. You can knock yourself out and cause a lot of pain (to yourself or others) when you forget to look within, but it's right there for the asking/taking. It's right there within you. And after a while, you get more practiced in opening it up till eventually the door stays unlocked, it stays wide open and you can cross back and forth whenever you please. In the world and out of it, you know, simultaneously. The great saints have accomplished this. The great Yogis of the Himalayas just sit there with the door wide open all the time, and you can hook up with that energy, any time, any place, 'cause it's right there within you, right there in the heart. You don't even have to sit and meditate for years on end, you just need to put your attention there. Be your own Yogi, be your own gatekeeper holding the key – it's you who unlocks it. It's you that opens the door, it's you who passes through it, and it's you on the other side (it's all you – good name for a song).

So that's all I'm going to say today – pick up the key on your way out – open the door – nice picture there – open door to the bliss of consciousness, eh?

We tried to picture it in Yellow Submarine – all the flowers popping up in the landscape, and the love. Hard to picture it, because it puts it into a contracted form, and bliss is pretty expanded – the molecules are pretty spread out – there's a lot of space in bliss.

Enjoy the day, spend the day with an open doorway – it's all yours for the asking/taking.
(let it be)
I send my love and blessings to you on this day
10/12/03
G. Harrison
Servant to Lord Krsna
ॐ +


**It isn't necessary** for us to work today since you're not feeling well (headache). Yes, you were right that your pain in the night bore some similarity to my own. Why does pain exist except to direct us toward God – a deeper place within us that gives us more strength than we have alone? Connect with that part of yourself, the divine seed within. Find strength in a higher power. Let go of the small, earthly ghost, a shell of impurity and dust. Go within to the treasured place of light and love in the heart. And feel better soon. Hare Krishna Hari Bol!

I am G. Harrison ॐ
10/14/03

**Here we are**, ready to begin again. So we were talking about the focus necessary to maintain God consciousness, weren't we? The inner focus on the heart, it seems to me. And that's where we can begin again today. There is so much in the world to pull your attention of seeming importance. The reality is that what APPEARS significant is there only to feed the ego – it's more significant to maintain the focus within which promotes peace. This means a great deal of discrimination – knowing what's necessary, and what isn't. If you think, well, anyone could take my place, my presence isn't important here, well, then it's not really necessary, is it? But if you think – this is something only I can provide, then you are tapping into soul purpose and reality as we prefer knowing it. And really, that's the question – The answer will determine whether something will feed you energy (tapping into Universal Consciousness) or siphon energy away (tapping into the worldly energy). Always ask yourself the question to determine what is Right Action.

Of course you'll find there are little bits of necessary activity, pulling you away from your focus, and this is just practice in pulling yourself, or your attention back to the core or the essence of the One True God within Us All. But overall, you can use this primary question to inquire the appropriateness of the action for you at any particular time. So I wish you the best of days. Love each one for its own sake – part being In the Moment, as you say. Celebrate the BEINGNESS of each and every conscious, waking moment and dedicate them all to Lord Krsna, to Christ, to the higher purpose, whatever you choose to call That Aspect of Being.

Blessings to the one and all,
I am servant to Lord Krsna
Geo Harrison
10/17/03
ॐ +


**Namaste!** Hari Bol! You've made it back. All is well, as they say – not to worry now. All is progressing as it needs to – Why do you think it's all happening – it's the contrast of light and dark – the knowledge (awareness) that God exists BEYOND the pain, beyond the darkness, beyond the clouds the sun is shining – too much of a good thing is illusionary, always there's a play between the darkness and the light. Seek the light and know it's eternal – the darkness fades away. Go in peace, child and know there are great beings beside you – above you/below you – remember God, remember all that you know inside yourself and be free.

I am Geo Harrison
11/12/03
ॐ

**Note:** my mother had been diagnosed with Alzheimer's in October, so I had been unable to keep up with the regular communication.

**Welcome back,** child, I've missed you! Hari Bol! We will resume where we left off – was it already a year ago? From here time appears different – it is not that it doesn't exist at all, only is an altered concept from yours (or where you are). The light serves to move this energy along different pathways and so we experience "time" in a simultaneous manner, rather than linear. Still, by watching movement on the earth plane, we can perceive the movement of events along those linear parameters.

The reason we are back in touch – no, I know you never went away, only became distracted, is that there is a series of messages which must come through at this time and since we (I) find you in a receptive state at present, you will receive them. Sit when you can – don't force it, just allow the information to come when necessary, and the messages will come through. I thank you from the bottom of my heart for your devotion – none of it was (or is) wasted. All energy is to be cherished as a manifestation of the One, of whatever Name you choose. We are, in fact, all One. All energy is One, and so when you send this energy from the Heart, it is noticed, it is perceived - and so it continues to be (because no energy ever goes away) it is only transformed.

Hari Bol. Om Tat Sat. Jaya Gurudev!

I am Geo. Harrison, this day
August 29, 2004
ॐ

**Note:** This was the last communication. I should also say that I did not alter these messages – they appear as they were received, unedited.

## Circle Spirits of the Indigenous Grandmothers

**Blessings, child** – it would behoove you to write these things down. Welcome to our spiritual circle. We are the ones who surround the grandmothers with light (The 13 Indigenous Grandmothers). We carry the vibration of their wisdom to all the world to hear and see, to feel and absorb. It is time now, as you yourself have spoken, for this planetary shift of consciousness. You have prepared yourself well to receive these energies into your own conscious awareness. Allow the energies we project to work through you. Simply follow the path as laid out for you – no need to artificially hasten it, for it has its own time schedule. When invited to speak, speak. When invited to tell, tell. When invited to show the way, show the way. It is all that is required at this time. You **will** find, however that these opportunities will increase, for you will be recognized as a holder of this exquisite energy, and those who hear of it will want to know. We say, simply stay in close proximity to your own spirit, and the information will flow easily.

Tonight, simply give an introduction. Tell of the grandmothers' different spirits, but bring attention to the fact that they are One Body, have formed an Alliance of Spirit and move together as one with One Purpose, One Calling, One Prayer – to heal the world of its ills, to bring it back to Oneness, and to establish the balance of peaceful co-existence.
We are all one.

We are all one.
We are all one.

Namaste. Walk in peace, child.

We are the Spirits of the Circle on this day of October 20, 2004

**O child, be at peace with yourself** – all will unfold in its own time, no need to hasten anything. The mind gets busy when we are out of sync with time, with the **present** moment, which is a **gift**, is it not? That supreme awareness of the **now** is all that is necessary. All else will follow! Do you understand? (Yes) And so we say to you at **this time** that you will be called upon from time to time to speak of the wisdom of the 13 indigenous grandmothers. It is your duty to contemplate their connection to whomever you meet, for there is a message for each and every one. Sometimes the message will be conveyed through words, sometimes energetically, sometimes through words and pictures, sometimes by pictures alone. Be aware of the words and images that come to you. Do not disregard any of them, for you ARE A CONDUIT OF THIS ENERGY now and will need to remain consciously aware of carrying it not only for yourself, but for others, and collectively, for the Whole, for the world.

It is for this reason that it is **I M P E R A T I V E** (we cannot stress this enough) to sit in meditation every morning, and before you speak (if possible) in order to maintain this connection, this awareness. Forgetfulness will not help – hence the grandmothers have stressed the importance of staying in a state of prayer. Go in peace and enjoy your day.

We are the Circle Spirits of the 13 Indigenous Grandmothers
October 21, 2004

**Good morning**, we feel you have entered a new realm of being, you will begin to see evidence of this shift – it is significant that your dear husband was present last evening in order to see the tremendous power of the Grandmothers' Circle. May it come to pass that he is ever more aware of this energy that it carries you forward to where you must go – and you must go. NEVER DOUBT THIS FOR AN INSTANT – ALL POINTS IN THIS DIRECTION. It is imperative that you build the basket as you were instructed at the Global Women's Gathering (13 Indigenous Grandmothers) in October. It is time to move forward as your new year begins. You will do this in a step-by-step practical way. No resistance will be met. Have faith in knowing that this is coming to pass - envision it, picture it, embrace it, know it to be true.

We are happy, we are delighted to announce that your career energy will now also unfold. You will be able to present your work in new and dynamic ways – remember the idea of the Mother within, for she will carry you where you need to go, as you will carry the mother without.

Know in your heart that you are living your path as it is destined to be lived – it is NO ACCIDENT that you are returning to your roots after having spent 30 years developing into your spiritual mastery. It is time now to ground that work in your home territory. Walk in peace and know we are with you.

We are the Circle Spirits of the Indigenous Grandmothers
12/31/04

# The Angels

**Remember, all is as it should be –** nothing is out of sync, all flows rhythmically as it should, only resistance offers the *illusion* of disequilibrium. Balance and harmony are yours AT ALL TIMES simply by letting loose of such resistance to the Flow of Life, the movement of the Shakti within all beings, within all things – sentient and insentient – we all know you understand this. You are tapping into the essence of life, the blood flow, if you will, of the ALL. Feel its pulse – coming and going, ebbing and flowing, as it breathes through All, pulsates with life. Remember to observe this throughout your day and bring the constant wonderment of its blessing. There are no mysteries, all is clear before you, simply take each step in this awareness as it unfolds before you. Enjoy its gifts as they are presented. You will always know the right moment for action for you will already be moving! Nothing stops and starts, there is simply this coming and going, this ebbing and flowing – inhale and exhale, but this flow of life never stops, it is in constant motion – even in its resting state, it is still part of this movement, this flow. Enjoy each day as it is presented (gifted) to you. Act accordingly. This is where the joy resides. This is where the life force is shared. This is where you find the Divine – in each and every moment of Being, in each and every moment of Life, in each and every moment of Bliss. So go in peace in this Supreme Awareness and know the Truth in this way –

We are Alandriel and Galadriel, servants to the One in all things.
10/23/04


**We are here at this time of your new year.** These are Momentous Times, are they not? Great Changes are taking place upon the Planet. At This Time that we speak – huge shifts of electromagnetic energy are occurring. Stay open and aware of all you sense and see – these changes will guide you in your decisions in the time to come. This weather pattern you are experiencing is an indication of this change. NEVER DOUBT that these changes are Underway NOW in this moment of time. It is so. A new world is being born, a new way of life and living is upon us.

Human beings will need to seek, and seek, a different way of being on and interacting with the planet and see that this planet is not isolated unto itself, but an integral part of the Cosmos beyond, much like a cell is an integral part of the body as a whole, and the body responds to and is responsible to those beyond it as well. This is a large system we/you are a part of. You humans glimpse only one fragment of the whole, which is why we say the vision of God in his/her totality is an AWESOME sight, beyond your senses to perceive, beyond your intellectual capacity to comprehend, beyond your ability to know. Those of you who are gatekeepers have an inkling of what it is we say, you have had experiences which offer some notion of what lies beyond the Gate, but it is only a small piece of the whole. All of life will/is come/coming to know of this Vastness of Being which lies before you. The Earth changes taking place now are opening that Gate wider so that you may see more, and so our worlds may merge. You are rising to a higher level of consciousness – you, who hold this energy, the gatekeepers, will be called upon more and more to raise the vibratory level so that those who reside on the planet can contain more energy – it will be ESSENTIAL to contain more energy so that the Ultimate Change can take place in years to come. YOU WILL BE PLACED WHERE YOU NEED TO BE. IT IS BEYOND YOUR CONTROL, SO DO NOT WORRY. Events will take place in your personal life which will make the change/movement possible. NO ONE WILL BE ABLE TO STAND IN THE WAY OF THESE CHANGES – survival will depend on it. You may say that this sounds a bit drastic in its nature – do not be frightened. It will simply appear as your next step, without a doubt. So we would say to hold the faith. Your own circle will expand in spite of the APPEARANCE of any delay. There is, in fact, no delay – all is happening at the appropriate time.

We would like to say, with all of our hearts, that we have certainly enjoyed (and expect to enjoy for eons to come!) working with you and your blessed energy. Your astute faculties sense these changes – you are indeed a sensitive, and one of our favorite ones to be working with at this time for the quality of your receptive abilities. Continue to serve Maker in this way – all gifts of the Universe shall be yours as you walk along this exalted path of service to the Divine One of All – you are our blessed one now and always.

In love and devotion, we are the servants to Lord Michael on High and pleased to be with you.
~Alandriel and Galadriel

Walk in peace, dear one.
January 1, 2005

# 3

## Teaching and Expressive Arts

I arrived at Expressive Arts on an unusual path. I started out as a preschool teacher - after graduating Cornell with a degree in Human Development, certified to teach nursery school and kindergarten, I opened my own school. The philosophy of the N-K Program at Cornell was that we were meeting the needs of the whole child – social, emotional, physical, and cognitive. Throughout the process of teaching, though, I had a nagging feeling that there was something more. I wanted to go deeper with the teaching and felt it was missing a spiritual component, but I didn't know how to achieve that. I was also making art in the afternoons, and after two years, decided that I was an artist and gave up the school (typical of an artist to move on to a new project when the creative energy hits).

As my art developed, I joined a group called Women's Caucus for Art, which supported the work of women artists and artists of color who were under-represented in the art world. I co-designed a regional conference at Yale that allowed one hundred women artists to show and speak about their work. I wanted to model what it could be like when conference attendees were active participants, rather than passive listeners as most conferences were designed. Through WCA, I met women who were involved in No Limits for Women Artists, an international network of women's support groups, working with a model devised by Betsy Damon after seeing that her peers came up against an invisible wall in their careers as artists. Upon examination, Betsy realized that they were stopping themselves from really going for their goals because of internalized sexism, racism, classism, homophobia, anti-Semitism, etc. They were telling themselves the messages that society had told them - that as women, their work was less important; as women of color, their work shouldn't be seen; as poor women, there were better ways to spend your money than on art supplies, and so on.

I became a No Limits leader, always having twelve women in my group. If someone dropped out, another would show up to take her place. I did this for several years and saw how the process was effective. My group members started moving towards their largest visions. However, the model was based on Re-evaluation Counseling, which had what I felt was an aggressive component. You could push a participant to their emotional breaking point to release what was holding them back. This did not sit well with me. I had not been abused in my childhood as some of the network members had been and was uncomfortable with this dynamic.

Around the time I became involved in No Limits, I went back for my master's degree in Humanistic Education with an emphasis in Women's Studies, at the State University of New York at New Paltz. I had decided that I wanted to work with women, and although I would not be able to counsel women individually, I could run groups (since that time I've realized I can work with individual women under the umbrella of education - hence my "unusual path"). I met Lucy Barbera who was in the program with me and was actually my daughter Juda's preschool teacher; Lucy also received certification through Natalie Rogers' Person-Centered Expressive Arts Institute in California - Natalie was the daughter of renowned humanistic psychologist Carl Rogers who developed the person-centered approach to therapy. Around the time I was establishing my No Limits group, I started doing some individual sessions with Lucy, experiencing expressive arts techniques which she had learned from Natalie's Institute. When I became extremely uncomfortable with the bullying techniques of No Limits, having experienced it firsthand at a No Limits regional workshop (one of the co-leaders of the network bullied me during a session with my group members present), I was able to do a training with Natalie Rogers. I realized Expressive Arts was the missing piece: we could access the inner information and emotion in a gentler way. I left No Limits (after being offered a hierarchical regional position) and developed Winternight WAVE: Women Artists Visionary Experience, which used the No Limits model, but with Expressive Arts. In time, I also started working with girls, age 9-11, calling it Girl's WAVE: We are Very Expressive.

Expressive Arts modalities include working with clay, collage, drawing and painting, making sound, creative movement, and meditation, among others. The idea is that we can use the art media without pre-conception, allowing ourselves free reign without judgment from ourselves or others, by simply seeing what happens. This fosters the ability to create an inner focus and intuition. We don't need others to interpret the meaning of our expression – we can do that for ourselves. Natalie Rogers added the Expressive Arts to her father Carl's model, realizing that if you piggy-backed the various modalities, one after the other, the participant's process deepened, allowing more information and personal meaning. She called this the Creative Connection™ which was also the name of her first published book.[8]

I ran a WAVE group for many years, offering workshops at my home as well as at various conferences, including presenting at CHARTS in the UK, which focused on healing in the arts, sponsored by Richard Attenborough. I began teaching at New Paltz in 2001, and in time taught some of Lucy Barbera's Expressive Arts courses, which she had developed and implemented at New Paltz by that time, eventually taking over for her entirely in 2019 and rewriting the courses to bring them into alignment with my own model and philosophy.

If I could go back now, I might have decided to pursue a master's degree in Counseling and integrated that with Expressive Arts. There are many graduate programs now that did not exist in those days. Keep in mind, though, that I am an artist and have maintained an active art career. I decided this was the right path for me, and now that I have one hundred fifty Expressive Arts students a year, I feel as though my original impulse towards education has been realized with that "something more." I should also add that I've had a strong spiritual practice since my 20's, which has informed my teaching. As a student of Swami Muktananda, I learned Siddha Yoga meditation and a rich philosophy of self-realization. All these

---

[8] Rogers, Natalie. *The Creative Connection*. Palo Alto, Science & Behavior Books, 1993.

elements came together to be integrated and synthesized into who I am and what I do now. We are multidimensional beings, after all.

## Expressive Arts Practices

As I've contemplated what Expressive Arts modalities to include here, what is coming through for me are what I'll call the Three M's: meditation, mandalas, and movement. Honestly, there are so many rich practices in Expressive Arts which help the participant to find deep inner meaning in their lives, but for our purposes, these are the ones I'll focus on here. I'll include a few more in the Expressive Arts Sessions later.

## Meditation

My feeling about meditation is that it should be done regularly, just as you would develop any practice, whether that be a musical talent like playing the piano or any other developing skill. Doing it at the same time everyday builds it into your schedule, making it a priority. Sit in the same spot each time, preferably a space you only use for the purpose of meditation, and either wear the same clothing or use something like a scarf or shawl, which you only use for this purpose. The meditation energy builds up in that location and in those articles of clothing, making it easier to develop an inner focus.

1. **Begin by getting comfortable**, sitting on a chair or a cushion, with your back straight so that the meditation energy *(Shakti* or *Kundalini)* can move easily up and down the spine *(shushumna)*.

2. **Close your eyes**, being aware of any tension you're holding in the body, and as you begin to focus on the breath, be sure to let go of anything you're holding onto. There is a common misconception that meditation is for the purpose of relaxation – certainly, that is a side effect of meditation, but the true purpose is to get to know the inner self.
3. **Notice the rising and falling of the breaths and notice where the inbreath meets the outbreath**, and vice versa. Just focus on that spot. It is the entry way into the inner self. My experience is that as I focus on that place between the breaths, the spot or space expands – it opens wider. I become absorbed in my inner being. Some people tend to expand at the top of the breathing cycle, others the bottom. It doesn't matter which. Don't force it – it's a natural process.
4. **The way you hold your hands** is a matter of preference, whatever works for you. Simply place your hands in your lap or putting the thumbs and index fingers together (*gyan* or *jnana*), will help you to focus in the third eye, between the eyebrows. If you touch the middle finger and thumb (*apana* or *prana*), the experience is more heart centered.
5. **Focus your attention on the third eye** between the eyebrows as you continue to breathe. Using a mantra will help discipline your attention as you breathe. It's the nature of the mind to think. Don't try to stop your thoughts or believe that you're not meditating if you're thinking. Just notice it, let the thought go, and re-focus on the breath, no matter how many times you must. Eventually, it becomes second nature. In the same way, do not be concerned about outside noises – simply acknowledge their presence, and refocus on the breath.

**I like to use a quartz crystal.** Quartz amplifies energy, and I find that it helps me to attune to the meditation energy. I simply hold it in one hand. Once you've done this for a while, experiment with moving the crystal up or down the body and observe the change in effect. For example, holding it at the heart will feel different as it amplifies the heart chakra energy.

## Meditation Variations

Once you've become comfortable with the basics of meditation, here are a few guided meditations that my students enjoy, which can be combined with Expressive Arts afterwards if you choose. If you want, you can record these directions, reading them **s l o w l y** and pausing after each step...

## Earth Meditation

Sit comfortably and breathe...send some roots down from the base of your spine or feet into the core of Earth...take some time to connect with Earth energy. Imagine yourself embraced by Earth - safe, content, secure, and nourished by Her energy. She protects you as if you are a small seed waiting to be burst forth. You are nurtured and protected. Feel her energy surround you...

When you're ready, send the energy back up the roots to your root chakra and know you are safe, secure, balanced and well protected. Wiggle your hands and feet, and when you're ready open your eyes.

## White Light Meditation

Enter your meditative state. Imagine a ball or sphere of brilliant white light above your head – this is your soul star, the halo we see depicted in paintings.

Allow the top of your head to open (crown chakra) to receive the white light; see it fill the crown of the head.

Let the energy move down to the third eye, between the eyebrows. See the third eye open and fill with the light.

Move the energy down to the throat and see the throat open to receive this light.

Move the light down to the heart chakra and see the heart open, filling with this brilliant white light. Allow the energy to move down the arms, into the hands and the fingertips, and beyond the fingertips...Then return to the heart.

Allow the energy to move down to the solar plexus, just below the rib cage (your gut). The solar plexus opens to receive the light. Breathe in, and as you out-breathe, allow any tension to fall away. You can even imagine the white light purifying your solar plexus, clearing out any old debris. Every organ is filled with light.

Move the energy down to the sacral chakra, just below the navel. See the sacral chakra open and fill with light. The entire abdomen fills with the white light.

Again, move the energy down, this time to the root chakra at the base of the spine. See the root open and fill with light. Now just notice you are lit up from the top of your head to the base of your spine.

Move the energy down the legs, through the knees, the ankles, and feet, and send it down some roots into the Earth, connecting with the core of Earth.

## Chakra Meditation

Start with the white light meditation, followed by some time feeling the Earth energy surrounding you, nourishing and protecting you.

Move the energy upwards, through the roots, the feet and ankles, and knees, arriving at the root chakra at the base of the spine. This time see the root chakra lit up with a brilliant **red** light. This is your connection to the Earth, your physicality – being in the body, your sense of safety and security, and balance. Feel yourself grounded in Earth energy.

Move the energy upwards to the sacral chakra, below the navel, this time lit up with a brilliant **orange** light. This is the center of your creativity – your ability to birth anything you wish in this life. Feel the potency of the sacral chakra, it's power to create.

Now move the energy upwards to the solar plexus, filled with a **golden yellow** light. This is the center of emotion – E motion, energy motion, your intuition, your gut. Feel the energy of the solar plexus, filled with this light.

Move the energy upwards once again, arriving at the heart, with an **emerald green** glow. Imagine that within the heart, there is a room – a chamber. You can decorate your heart chamber anyway you wish… There is a seat for your soul to sit upon, and you sit down upon the seat. There's a knock at the door and you rise to answer it. You open the door, and there standing in the doorway is your guide. What do they look like? How are they dressed? Who is it? Perhaps they will tell you their name… Invite your guide into your heart chamber, to sit next to you on your seat. If you have a question that you'd like to ask your guide, go ahead and do it now, and receive the answer…

Allow the energy to rise into the throat chakra, this time with a **cobalt blue** light. See the throat open and fill with this brilliant blue light, soothing, healing, and opening. This is your ability to express yourself, to speak your truth.

The energy rises to the third eye, between the eyebrows, filled with an **indigo** light. This is your ability to see where you are going, to see your direction. Where are you headed? If you wish, you can imagine where you'll be 5 years from now…what do you see?

Allowing the energy to rise again, this time to the top of the head, lit up with a **violet** light, this is your spirit – who you are in this lifetime – the essence of you. Feel yourself and who you are.

And again, rising to the soul star, the ball of white light above the head, your connection with All that Is, higher consciousness, soul. **

Now see the white light surround you and move down through you, passing through each energy center, and down through the roots into the Earth, reconnecting with Earth energy.

Slowly, come back into the body, wiggle your hands and feet, and open your eyes when you're ready.

**If you wish, you can continue upwards…allow the energy to rise 12-14 inches above the head, to a 7th dimensional energy, the angelic realm. Picture what it is you want to create in your life, see it projected on a screen… Now collapse the energy quickly, sending it downwards through each energy center, and down into the Earth. And the Universe responds, Yes…

Take your time to open your eyes.

## Making Art after Meditation

You don't have to be an artist to make art. In Expressive Arts, there's no judgment, only expression. If you want to continue the meditation energy, find the mediums you most enjoy – markers, oil pastels, chalk pastels, watercolors, or acrylic paints. My favorite is using oil pastels, and then putting a thin wash over it – either watering down the acrylics or tempera paint or using watercolors. There's no right way to do it, just express the energy you saw, felt, or feel afterwards. Let go of the notion that it needs to look a certain way or be controlled – free-expression is the key here. Just play!

Put on some meditative, instrumental music.

## Mandalas

Circles occur in Nature and in every culture upon the planet. A mandala is simply a sacred circle, used to focus our attention. One sees them in front of Hindu and Buddhist temples as a way of focusing inwards. I find they are particularly satisfying after meditation, when I can draw or paint what I saw or felt. Here's one I made with chalk (soft) pastels. Afterwards, I allowed the words to come to me without thinking.

*Exploration of light energy, tentative, yet assured, that where it leads is to the Source within*

The psychoanalyst Carl Jung used mandalas with his patients in the early 1900's, as well as doing them himself. He believed that the mandalas his patients created were windows into their souls. I prefer less traditional mandalas, embracing more artistic ones.

### Making a Mandala

Trace a big circle on a piece of paper – use a plate or a pot lid – bakery circles work too. Choose your medium, put on some meditative music, and explore the energy. Do some free writing afterward – whatever comes to mind.

### Creative Movement

The Ones have said that it's important to embody the new energies entering the planet's atmosphere right now. That means incorporating the energy into the body, absorbing it into every cell. We are changing physiologically – our DNA is altering; we are becoming updated versions of ourselves. Movement allows the incorporation of light into the body. Personally, I like to put on meditative music immediately after meditation and simply move to it. These are not prescribed movements as in yoga. They are impulses of movement from the inside out. This can take a completely free form, or you can explore each of the chakras. I always connect with the Earth first, honoring and invoking Her energy. Then I bring that energy upwards, through each chakra. You can explore only one chakra – I've spent weeks exploring the movement of only one chakra before moving onto the next; or you can move the energy through each of the chakras in turn, from bottom to top, as well as from above. Be sure to re-ground at the end.

### Find the right combination

If I were going to do a creative connection™ of all four of these modalities: meditation, drawing, movement, and free writing, I might play with the order to see which works best for me. I always like to start with meditation, but if I were doing it later in the day and was feeling some angst, I might start with movement to release the discomfort, then draw, then write, and then meditate. If I'm doing this first thing in the morning, which works best for me, I'd meditate, move, draw, and then write. It doesn't really matter as long as it has a flow. The idea is that you continue the energy from one modality to the next. You'll go deeper with each one. Finishing with free writing helps to make meaning or sense out of the experience.

## Sound and Movement

What I call 'sound & movement' is a good way to tap into and release internal energy, feelings, or emotions. After answering the questions (see Expressive Arts Sessions), stand up, close your eyes, and tune into your gut. Then bring out an *authentic* sound and physical movement to release it. I say authentic because it's not a cerebral exercise – not *oh, what should I do?* but instead, *how do I feel?* It can also be used at the end of your Expressive Arts session to express what you're feeling – positive or challenging. The more we can tune into the way we're feeling, the greater our capacity for developing intuition and our inner guidance system.

## Creating Change

Change is a creative process, which is why using Expressive Arts to get your creative juices flowing helps immensely. When we are disturbed or dissatisfied with some aspect of our lives, we can discover what we would prefer through some self-reflection. Anything we can do to enhance that self-reflection will be helpful, requiring a more intuitive rather than rational approach. Identifying and letting go (releasing) what no longer works for us, gives us the space in our lives to do something else or do what we have been doing in a new way. Identifying what excites us indicates the direction we can take.

Even small changes can be life-altering. Think of a blue cube. Each side of the cube is blue. If you make one side red, it's suddenly no longer a blue cube. You didn't have to change the whole thing, just one aspect to make a difference.

Some folks get fearful of the idea of change, thinking it must be something major or that they will somehow lose themselves in the process. You cannot lose yourself – you take yourself wherever you go. All your talents and skills go with you – these are the superpowers you can rely on. Everybody's got them. The change doesn't need to be a major leap; it can be small and gradual. Defining a very large vision can be intimidating, but taking it one step at a time is doable. We're always in a process of change, whether we know it or not – that's the nature of life. There are cycles which, if we're attuned to them, will help us to navigate the journey.

**Creation   Sustenance   Dissolution**

You start something new – a new job, a new practice, a new way of doing your art, a new work of art, moving to a new space, starting a new garden... Creativity takes many forms. Then you must sustain it...keep up the practice, maintain the garden, or whatever it takes to keep this new endeavor going. After a while, the energy starts to wane. This happens in Nature every year – spring brings new growth, the growth is sustained in the summer, and then in autumn, the energy starts to dissipate and eventually die. Dissolution is the natural falling apart that takes place in the life cycle – whether it's your life or a natural life cycle. The problem is that we don't always honor the falling apart. Instead, we resist it, clinging to old life forms that no longer work for us. Learning to let go is part of the process. In the world of numerology, we live in nine-year cycles, beginning anew in year one, and letting go in year nine. If we are attuned to the changes, we experience the natural ups and downs inherent in the process. When we resist, the Universe has a way of coming up behind us and kicking us in the pants, which is uncomfortable at best!

I often pose questions before Expressive Arts which allow students or WAVE participants that opportunity for self-reflection. You can journal the answers to these questions as well, though stating them out loud to another person lends them power, so you may want to find a partner to share the work. Here are some questions you can consider as you prepare yourself to enter a process of change.

- What's going well in my life?
- What's difficult or challenging?
- If I could change one thing, what would it be?
- What would I have let go to make that happen?
- What kind of support would I need?
- What are my strengths? Being able to speak this out loud is extremely empowering.
- What excites me? Am I doing that? If not, why not?

**The 4 No Limits Questions** (developed by Betsy Damon):

1. What's my largest vision for myself? Go as big as you want.
2. What's my next step?
3. Where does it get difficult? Identifying where it gets hard for you indicates what you might be believing about yourself that's holding you back.
4. Where can I find (unconditional) support to keep from getting stuck?

These questions can be revisited periodically, to refresh the vision, redefine the next step(s), and continue to clear out the beliefs that are holding you back from action. It's important to examine what we believe about our capabilities and contradict these limiting beliefs with ones that support our moving forward. They may sound like affirmations but are actually contradictions of limiting beliefs. Imagine I'm a woman struggling to make ends meet. I need to buy art supplies to make the paintings I want to. My limiting belief tells me I can't spend money on the canvases I need. My contradiction might be *the world wants my work; the money will come back to me*. Or perhaps I'm afraid of being seen, so I hesitate to market my work. The contradiction would be *my work will enhance the world*. I'm a bit nervous about how I'll publish this book, believing I don't know how to do that or won't succeed. My contradiction could be *I can find support to help me publish this book,* or *My guides will show me the way.* Once we change our thinking, it's easier to proceed.

## Manifestation

We are being told now that bringing through new situations in our lives will be easier than it was in the old paradigm. Manifestation will be easier. Keep in mind, we are manifesting all the time, but because of the old patterning of self-doubt and worry, we either block the process or manifest what we don't prefer! Florence Scovel Shinn was a spiritual teacher, especially active in New York City in the 1920's. She told her students to "act as if" – in other words, set the stage for success. Behave the way you would if the situation were already here. She also encouraged her followers to make strong, positive statements OUT LOUD, which would cut through any doubt or negativity that might prevent a desired goal of coming through: *Today IS the day of my amazing good fortune!*[9] My daughter Juda and I tested this out with great success in the gallery: *People are flocking to the gallery and paying large quantities of cash for our art!* On that day, we would only have cash sales, no credit cards!

Now that manifestation is easier, it's important to be clear on what you want – see the vision, make the statement, trust in guidance, and get out of the way! When you let go, you make way for the energy to come through. And the more receptive to inner guidance you are, the clearer your vision will be. There's a play here between action and receptivity (not passivity). In the old paradigm we had to work hard to manifest something – there was a lot of action which needed to be sustained over time. Also, I think people who thought that receptivity to guidance would magically make things happen didn't do enough to create the change. The reality is it's a balance between the two polarities: action and receptivity. Being receptive allows us to perceive what we want to create, what we want to do, and knowing when it's the right time to act! If we

---

[9] Scovel Shinn, Florence. *The Complete Works of Florence Scovel Shinn*. New York, Dover Publications, 2010.

can balance these two polarities, understand that it's not either/or, but an integration of the two, then we are at an advantage. My guides communicated early this year that in April, I'd be presented with new work. That took receptivity to perceive. On April 1st, I received my former student's email that sparked this writing. The action? To write the book; however, I remain receptive to guidance as I'm writing which has made this process a true pleasure. Polarity is a thing of the past – not that there aren't still opposites. When I started my first school, we read a book called *Push, Pull, Empty, Full* to the children.[10] The difference now is that we understand that you can't have one without the other – they are two sides of the same coin. They are each a piece of the whole. Oneness is the name of the game.

## Change…

I use this formula for change:

### Greater self-awareness + support + taking action ➔ change

As we come to know ourselves better through self-examination (Expressive Arts helps in this process), finding unconditional support (no judgment) and taking steps toward our vision, change develops. Notice there isn't an equal sign in the formula; instead, it's an arrow, indicating a *process* of creating change. What seems essential now as this planetary ascension develops, is that we are attuned to our new being – our new identity, making way for new growth and expression. As we bring through more soul energy now, our piece of the Whole is necessary on a more expanded level – it's no longer just about us as individuals, but us as a part of the Collective Whole. This formula will work for us as individuals, yes. But it's also applicable to the bigger picture, what we are becoming as a unified global community. Our collective self-awareness is deepening as we examine our values and their impact on all of us and all of Nature. New ways of supporting each other's growth are emerging, and we are taking action on a broader scale than ever before.

---

[10] Hoban, Tanna. *Push, Pull, Empty, Full*. Springfield, Collier Books, 1972.

## Doing the Work

Work is also taking on new meaning. Drudgery is out, joy is in. If you're dragging the dead weight of past experience with you, it will feel like hard work. If we are engaging our higher level being into the process, it feels more like play. First, we must release the old patterning, so that we can engage the joy. But that process of letting go doesn't need to feel like work! Playing with art materials and moving our bodies allows this growth to take place in a more pleasurable way – not that shadow work is necessarily joyful, but engaging our creativity and expression can ease the way. I recently read a student's paper in which he said the activities of the past weeks had been "fun!" My first reaction was, well, we're working on our fears and shadow material, facing our internal demons – how is that fun?? But then I realized that dealing with the issues in a playful way allowed him to examine the difficult energies with a childlike energy. Keep in mind also that starting new endeavors isn't always easy. The I Ching would label this "difficulty at the beginning." We must be patient with ourselves, be compassionate toward ourselves, and understand that change is a process, not a destination.

## Focusing

As I've said, releasing or letting go the emotions and beliefs blocking your way is going to be essential, not just for communicating with your guides, but in manifesting what you want to create in your life. Eugene Gendlin was a humanistic psychologist and a contemporary of Carl Rogers. He noticed that some clients were successful in creating change in their lives and others weren't – they might get in touch with feelings, but nothing shifted. Upon closer examination, he recognized a process, which he named *Focusing*,[11] happening automatically in these successful clients, and wrote about the 6-step process. He noticed that as these people talked about what was troubling them, they would

---

[11] Gendlin, Eugene. *Focusing*. New York, Bantam Books, 1978.

have a *felt sense* of the issue they were experiencing, be able to name or label it, and then receive information about its meaning. It was a way for them to attune to their own inner guidance. Here's how it might have worked in a person-centered therapy session: the client made a statement about their problem; the empathic therapist would restate the client's words in their own words and understanding; the client would pause to evaluate if that's what they had meant – that's when the *focusing* took place, an internal sensing of the issue: is that what I meant? If not, the client could restate the issue to clarify. When the client tuned into what Gendlin called the *felt sense* and labeled it, a physical release happened – a twitch, a yawn, a movement, the body's release of the stored energy. Once cleared, they were able to move on in their process of change. Here are Gendlin's six steps:

1. Sit quietly and clear some space in your head.
2. Think about the issue you're experiencing and scan the body for a *felt sense* of it. Is there a place in the torso that feels concentrated or heavy or stuck?
3. Name it (give it a label).
4. Check the name against the felt sense. Is it the right one? Does it match? If not, change it.
5. Ask yourself, what's difficult or significant about this?
6. Without analyzing, receive the information (writing it down helps).

I attest to the fact that this process works – I have tested it numerous times, and often do it in the shower in the morning. I'm cleaning the outside of myself; I might as well clean the inside! The process can be repeated immediately and more than once if you want to get to the heart of the situation and really want to clear out the old energy. You can continue until you don't sense it anymore.

## Expressive Arts Sessions

As Natalie Rogers wrote about in her book, the creative connection (her trademark), involves piggy-backing the Expressive Arts modalities. Here, I've designed a few sessions that you can utilize for personal and collective growth. Keep in mind, you can always develop your own; it simply means putting one modality after another, deepening the experience with each step. Don't forget, be as authentic in your expression as possible; let go of the need to control your expression or any pre-conceived idea of what it should look like. There's no right way, only *your* way. It's an exploration. Approach it that way. Something to remember is that we don't talk while doing Expressive Arts – we want to create an inner focus.

### Releasing #1

1. Close your eyes and clear some inner space, breathing out any tension you're feeling in your body. Think about an issue you're dealing with now.

2. Poses: Opening your eyes, stand up and put your body into a shape which FEELS like this issue, like a sculpture. Feel it from the inside out. Now imagine how you would feel if this issue were gone. Shape your body to represent that feeling. Again, feel it from the inside out. Repeat each pose: the issue and if the issue were gone.

3. Putting on some instrumental music, draw the feelings of this issue with oil pastels. Don't worry about what it looks like, just express the feelings. Let the colors call to you as they're needed. Be aware of your thoughts and feelings.

4. Do some free writing afterward, anything that comes to mind.

**Releasing #2**

1. Close your eyes and clear some inner space, breathing out any tension you're feeling in your body. Think about an issue you're dealing with now.

2. Option A. Using clay if you have some, just play with the clay for 7 minutes, without music. Let the clay shape itself without pre-conception, not making anything specific. You can pound it, tear it, push it, pull it... If a shape begins to emerge, follow it. Be aware of your thoughts and feelings as you work with the clay.

    Option B. If you don't have clay, put on some instrumental music; close your eyes (or keep a soft focus) and feel the issue. Begin to move your body, as you contemplate the issue. Continue moving until you feel you're done.

    Option C. *Melting & Growing*: put on some instrumental music and allow yourself to melt...letting go of the feelings surrounding this issue. You may find you reach the floor in this process. Melt until all the feelings are gone. When you're ready, reverse the process and grow upwards, feeling how it can be when you've left the issue behind. Repeat.

3. Now draw or paint the feelings from any of the options from step #2 you used. Just continue to explore the feelings and see what happens.

4. *Focusing*: Follow the 6-step process for *focusing*, as designed by Eugene Gendlin (see page 75).

5. Write: I'm realizing _____.

## Attuning

1. Close your eyes and breathe, letting go of any tension in the body. Follow one of the guided meditations, or simply meditate on your own.

2. Option A. Using some instrumental, meditative music, paint your experience – either what you felt or saw, or what you're feeling now.

   Option B. Draw a large circle on your paper and draw or paint a mandala, using the feelings from your meditation.

3. Continue using the music. Stand up and contemplate the drawing/painting. Move to it.

4. Either free write, whatever comes to mind, or write the drawing or painting's story. Another option is to begin with the prompt, *I am Spirit*…

## An Expression for Self

1. Close your eyes and clear some inner space…be sure to focus on the spot where the inbreath meets the outbreath… Then, focus on the Self. Who are you? What's your energy? What do you want to express? Take time to go deeply within to reflect on who you are. When you're ready, wiggle your hands and feet, and open your eyes.

2. Trace a large circle on your paper, and paint or draw a non-traditional mandala of the Self. I like to use Ravi Shankar sitar music for this.

3. Write the story of the Self. You can begin, "I am _____" if you wish.

## An Expression for the World (or the Earth)

1. Go within and connect with the inner self. Imagine yourself in the center of the world. Continuing with eyes closed, what energy do you give to the world or the Earth? Pause...What energy does the world, or the Earth give to you? Pause...When you're ready, wiggle your hands and feet, and slowly open your eyes.

2. Make an energetic or artistic mandala (use Ravi Shankar music).

3. When you're done, do some writing:

    Option A. Tell the world or Earth's story.

    Option B. Write a conversation between the Self and the Earth. What would they have to say to each other?

# 4
## Self as Artist

I drew as a child, as most children do. I loved making scenes of ice skaters in winter, which were illustrations of my own experience growing up in the north. I remember the colors I used for these pictures: magenta, turquoise, purple, and a bit of pink. When I was six, a picture was chosen for an exhibit at the Schenectady Museum. The difference between me and many others is that I never stopped drawing. Our school district had an excellent art program, and in high school I was able to take art classes and independent studies in art. When I got to college, I didn't take 'art' classes, but I did find a professor who seemed to live in the attic of the College of Agriculture in the university, wore a white lab coat, and let me make my illustrations without interference. Once or twice, he came by me (working alone in the lab), suggesting this or that color. That was it.

When I had the nursery school, I spent my mornings teaching and my afternoons drawing. It was not surprising that I declared myself an artist when I grew bored of teaching privileged children, and so the journey of becoming an Artist began.

I started with weaving tapestries in wool, reading about Navajo weaving and building simple frame looms. Interestingly, the earliest pieces were rather geometrical in form, inspired by a tree of life pattern I'd seen in the Edinburgh Botanical Gardens in Scotland. As my meditation practice deepened, the tapestries reflected that experience. I created prayer rug inspired pieces, always signed with an Om:ॐ. I didn't feel I could claim credit for the work – in a sense, I felt it was coming through me. However, by the late 70's, I was feeling like I needed to take myself more seriously as an artist, hence my decision to ask for a name in meditation.

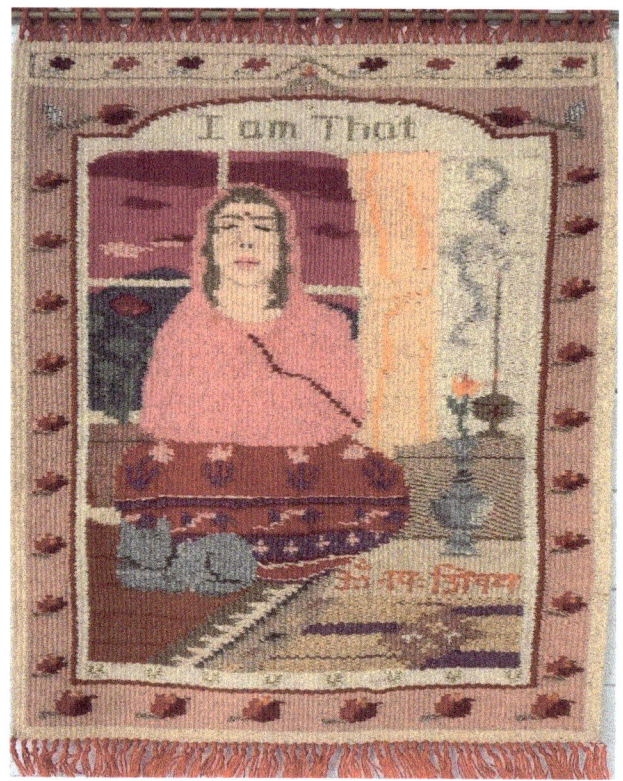

*I am That*, 40 x 30, woven tapestry in wool

     I sat on the floor with the frame loom leaning against the wall in front of me, playing Sanskrit chants from Baba Muktananda's ashram. The experience was meditative, so the lines between my spiritual life and my art were blurred. It was not surprising that in 1981, weaving a self-portrait in meditation in reds, oranges, and metallic gold (the colors associated with Shakti – the kundalini energy that rises in meditation and the female principle associated with Shiva), I had a vision of Baba's feet in his garden in Ganeshpuri, India. What I was doing was putting my experiences into pictures, woven in wool – not really any different from the crayon drawings from childhood, which reflected my experiences then.

After weaving tapestries for ten years, I developed a pinched nerve in my neck and was unable to continue. Here was the dilemma: how to be an artist without my 'art?' I still had my story to tell. After some deliberation, I began to paint. At first, I used oil paints – that's what Robert was using. I painted pictures of my domestic life: my children, my laundry, my garden... And then I was struck by inspiration like no other up to that point. I went to visit my friend Susan, who lived on a farm. I was sitting on the hillside, watching her hang her laundry on the clothesline. Very suddenly, I had a vision of her flying over her clothesline and simply said to myself: that's a painting! I went home and painted an 11 x 14 canvas of *Susan Take Flight* – Susan rising into the sky with the clothesline below. After that, I painted a large, 36 x 48 canvas, *Susan Moves On*. She was much further into the distance, high in the sky, the clothesline far below. These flying paintings soon became my genre. When people asked what my art was like, I simply said, I paint flying women. No one seemed to have heard of that before, except for Chagall's paintings. The subject matter was often still domestic. Usually the figures carried a dishtowel, which I felt represented their work as women in the world. Understand these paintings coincided with my more political awareness of women in the arts. Part of our work was to create transformation in our world – to make it more inclusive, to free ourselves from our oppression. Women's Caucus for Art allowed me to join this movement, and No Limits for Women Artists allowed me to transform myself as well as give other women tools to create change for themselves. The stronger our art, the stronger our voices, the greater the impact on our world.

Left: *Angel*, 9x12, oil on polymer panel, 1992  Right: *Out for an Airing*, 8x10, acrylic on board, 2018

At some point…in a painting called *Angel* from 1992, the flying woman sprouted wings. She was still flying above a clothesline, though in this painting she was taking the clothesline with her – taking her work out into the world. Now she was elevated - she flew in a deep midnight sky with stars, no ground visible. Since this was the time I was beginning to communicate with angels, more of my work reflected this level of awareness. The difference between the flying women and the angels was usually the color of the sky and whether the ground was visible or not. The women were still connected to the Earth, while the angels were high above. I call them 'the women,' but they were almost always me, depicting an experience I had, like a frozen moment of time. At some point, I changed to acrylic paints. They were easier to clean up, without the fumes. Otherwise, the subject matter remained the same: women flying above mountains or sea, angels high in the sky with stars, finally culminating in the *Winternight Trinity*. Since the completion of those three self-portraits (vertical figures, rather than the usual horizontal), the energy work has taken precedence. The energy mandalas are my only subject matter – a place beyond the stars.

I haven't spoken about my work as a professional artist, the career-focused part of me. Once I started taking myself more seriously as an artist, I began to show my work, either in solo exhibitions or group shows. One of the more notable shows was one Robert and I had together at, yes, the Schenectady Museum. There are times when the circle is completed, and this was one of them. And I still haven't mentioned my painted quilts – here my painting and love of fabrics and quilting came together. Robert and I were able to purchase an old house on Cape Breton Island, Nova Scotia, where we had been spending time in the summer since college. In our first summer at the house, I arrived with a herniated disc in my back and was unable to do my own framing, as I had grown accustomed to doing. I came up with the solution to paint on fabric and use dishtowels (teatowels in Canada) to cut up and sew around the paintings. If I didn't have the right color towel, a trip to the local discount store, where they had an extensive display of teatowels, provided me with what I needed. Hence, the painted quilt was born. These eventually developed into more sophisticated pieces. I did enjoy the process of combining fiber with painting, which incorporated the domestic element in my art.

Left: *Snowbird*, 18 x 20, painted quilt   Right: *Waiting for Spring*, 18 x 20, painted quilt

Twice, I've had a Winternight Gallery – a place to display and sell my art. But they've also been places for me to interact with visitors, for them to tell their stories and for me to tell mine. Often, people will tell me their flying dreams (more common than you think) after they see my flying women. I, myself, have had only two flying dreams in my life and only in the past decade. As I've said in my artist statements, it's more about the way I feel in my waking life. People will open to me about spiritual experiences that they might not tell any other person. This is a large part of who people are – some may say it's all of who they are. And yet, it's been a taboo subject for discussion for fear someone will think they're crazy. When more people begin to open about their sensory experiences, their visions, their inklings or intuition, it will free us to become more of ourselves – not just as individuals, but as a collective. Part of the spiritual experience is understanding the concept of Oneness. We are not isolated beings. We are essential parts of the Whole. What was it Sananda said? *Do not think of yourself as separate – you are a part of a divine network.* Art has been a vehicle for me to express my inner experience and for others to recognize theirs. Even art is not separate. It touches others, impacting their self-awareness as well as understanding the experiences of others. The more we can acknowledge each other, the stronger the understanding that we have shared human experiences; the more we acknowledge that, the more connected we feel...that sense of Oneness. *We're all in this together* takes on a larger, more significant meaning.

## Oneness

In contemplating the order of these sections: Channeling, Teaching, and Art, I decided to arrange them in the order of the *Winternight Trinity*. Although I experience them all simultaneously, the paintings arrived in a particular order, so I honor that here. How we choose to live our lives reflects our sense of purpose, what we arrived here on Earth to do, who we are as spirits and souls. It may be a lifelong process of discovering what that is, and now that we have entered a profound period of change, we may find our priorities are shifting – some aspects of ourselves are no longer current, others become more imperative. When we resist this transformation, there is discomfort, pain, and distress. It's necessary to find ways of letting go…and then opening to the new energies. Trusting in your inner guidance, trusting in yourself (you can never fall off yourself – you take your talents and skills with you on the journey), and trusting that you'll land where you need to be are essential in the process. Without risk there's no growth, and growth is rarely comfortable. Creating a vision of where you want to go in your life will take you there, and the vision becomes clearer as you tune into the inner self, taking cues from within. Where our visions overlap, like a myriad of Venn diagrams, is our co-creation. Each of us, contributing the fullest aspects of ourselves empowers this process. Talk about mandalas! Can you imagine such a work of art? That is Wholeness. That is Oneness. Step into the picture.

# 5

# Balance, Integration, Synthesis

### Balance

Let's face it. Life can be busy and challenging. Back in the 90's, with all that I was doing inside and outside of the house, I developed a system to help me stay mindful of the work that needed to be done – the places I wanted to put my energy, and the places I was putting it. It's hard to keep that all in your head and not keep thinking about it all. What I came up with was something I call a *Winternight House Diagram*™. Imagine a house – any kind of house you want, with each room of the house representing one aspect of your life or one overall category, your goals in the attic, a foundation of the values you believe in, and a compost pile outdoors for all the stuff that no longer serves you, whether that be stress or negativity or something in your life you simply want to let go. You can refine it; you can re-draw it daily, or weekly, or whenever you simply want to take inventory in your life. What the *Winternight House Diagram* gives you is a visual representation of who you are and what you do, clarity about how you want to live your life as well as how you have been living it. In addition, I wrote my next tasks in each of the categories or rooms to highlight what I needed to attend to.

I discovered that I live in a 4-room house: Teaching, Self, Home & Family, and Art. My attic contained my purpose of helping others to fulfill themselves and fulfilling myself – inspiring others and inspiring myself – always two-fold. My foundation was built on creativity, expression, integrity, and so on. When I shared this model with other women, I realized that some women lived in one-room houses, often without an attic, and others lived in hotels. The ones who lived in one room were often depressed. They only served the needs of their families, having nothing of their own, and it was difficult for them to see how they could move out of that funk – hence no attic. Once an attic was built on, there was a sense of hope and possibility. The women who lived in hotels had too much going on, and it was hard to focus. Everything had its own category – food shopping, kids, driving the kids, doing their art, showing their art, creativity, designing a garden, planting the seeds, cooking, etc. etc. etc. I noticed these women often suffered from A.D.D. If they combined tasks into overall categories – for example, Home & Family, which incorporated the cooking, cleaning, shopping, and gardening…or Art, incorporating all its aspects, not only would life feel more organized, but be more manageable because they could now focus; stuff got done.

    The house diagram also serves as a tool for balance in one's life. Often one room can take precedence, so that something like self-care falls by the wayside. If there's a room for self-care (mine contained meditation, walking, eating well, etc.), then one must pay attention to it. One can see where one's energy is going and be sure to distribute one's energy more evenly. Now this isn't to say that you can do everything at once. I might spend an intense week reading student papers, which means that the next week I may focus more in my studio to balance myself. I can also take a walk in the middle of the paper-reading to replenish my energy. By organizing myself visually, I can find the balance that gives me a sense of both accomplishment and well-being. One of my favorite quotes is from educator Jerome Freiberg: *organization is the foundation*.

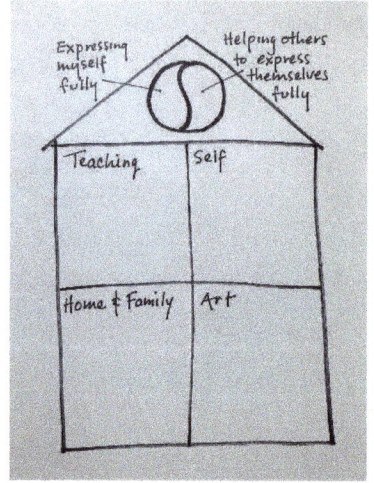 

Left: *Winternight House Diagram*, ink  Right: oil pastel & watercolor

## Making a House Diagram

My house diagram is more traditional, reflecting the shape of the house I live in. Others find different shapes to work well; I have one friend whose house diagram is circular. Here are some questions to ask yourself before you draw (or paint) your diagram:

1. What are the areas where I put my energy? Make a list. These will be your **rooms.**
2. Are there any areas that can be combined to simplify my list? The fewer rooms, the more easily you'll see where to put your energy.
3. What are my overall goals? Keep it simple – you can place smaller goals in the individual rooms. This is your **attic.**
4. What supports my life? In other words, what gives me a sense of safety and security, and what values do I live by? You may want to place the people who offer you (unconditional) support here as well. This is your **foundation.**

5. What do I want to let go? What's no longer useful for me or blocks my progress or ability to focus? These are the things that will end up in your **compost**.

Once you've completed this list, draw the house. Remember, it can be any shape or configuration you want – after all, it's your house! Some variations of this are using oil pastel to draw and label the house, then use a watercolor wash over it – the oil pastel will show through. Or you can paint with acrylics. You may find that the images are more representational or symbolic rather than specifically labeled – whatever has meaning for you.

**Alternative: make a collage.** Cutting out magazine words and images, and using a glue stick, make a collage of your house diagram. Let the words and images call to you, rather than looking for specific ones.

### Integration

With the passage of time, I realized that the energies of these rooms don't always stay in their neat little compartments. My art is influenced by my meditation, my teaching by my art, my art by my relationship with my daughter – I had a show of paintings in her atelier that incorporated my flying women with her fashion design. My teaching and art combine when I design lesson plans or workshops. This means that the walls in my room are not necessarily solid but allow flow of energy from one to another, which allows me to use more of my skills, more of talents in any endeavor.

Before we can think about how our rooms interact, we must have defined each one individually. The *I Ching* says, *In order to find one's place in the infinity of being, one must be able to both separate and unite*: seeing yourself as a separate entity as well as an integral part of the whole.[12] Before we can know

---

[12] Baynes, Wilhelm. *I Ching: Book of Changes*. Princeton, Princeton University Press, 1967.

ourselves in our entirety, we need to know the parts, just as before we can know the Whole of the Universe, we must know the entirety of ourselves. Remember the image of our overlapping Universal Venn diagram? We can't see that picture in its entirely until we see our complete individual piece. We are whole beings comprised of various parts.

Here are some questions to think about:

1. How do the rooms of my house interact or influence each other?
2. Do I spend equal time in each room? If not, why not?
3. Is there one room where I need to put more of my energy to feel more whole?
4. What can I incorporate in my house diagram to give me a greater sense of wholeness, ease, or well-being?
5. Who am I as a whole, integrated being? Write as if you're thinking out loud – you don't need to know the answer!

### Mind Maps

After working with some clients or group participants, I began to understand that their brains may operate differently from mine. Organization is easy for me. I'm able to focus readily and can create well-defined areas of my life. I've worked to create boundaries with family members to provide this for myself, and I think my brain's left, analytical side is balanced with its right, intuitive side. My real house (not the house diagram) is well-organized – everything has a place, and I know where most things are at any given moment. My house reflects who I am (except for the parts I share with my husband who is less organized, but that's a story for another day). The women I'm referring to who operate differently, have cluttered lives – their houses contain too many objects, too many papers, too many collectibles, too much unsorted trash. The result is chaos, and their attention is scattered. But their living spaces reflect their minds, their inner states, as mine does. I can't say to them, do it my way and your life will miraculously change. They don't function in the same way. In fact, I'd say they tend to be more creative, more spatially intelligent learners. What I've discovered in the process of teaching diverse learners, is that a tool like a **mind map** can offer these women a way to see their whole life. They can see the scattered threads as being connected in some way, can understand that they experience much simultaneously. Rather than labeling them with A.D.D., maybe we can give them effective tools which help them to function on their own terms and see that rather than a disability, they have an *extra* strength or ability. A mind map is a picture they can truly understand - life suddenly makes sense. As a more linear thinker, it was difficult for me to draw a mind map at first– I had to learn to do it. But it helped me to grasp what these women experience. Because the areas of these women's lives begin more integrated than a linear thinker's, this tool seems to help them to perceive all parts at once.

Here are some guidelines for making your own mind map. The first important principle is to use as much color as possible. I find colored markers to be helpful. Also, as many visual images that can be incorporated will reinforce the information – spatial learners respond to color and pictures.

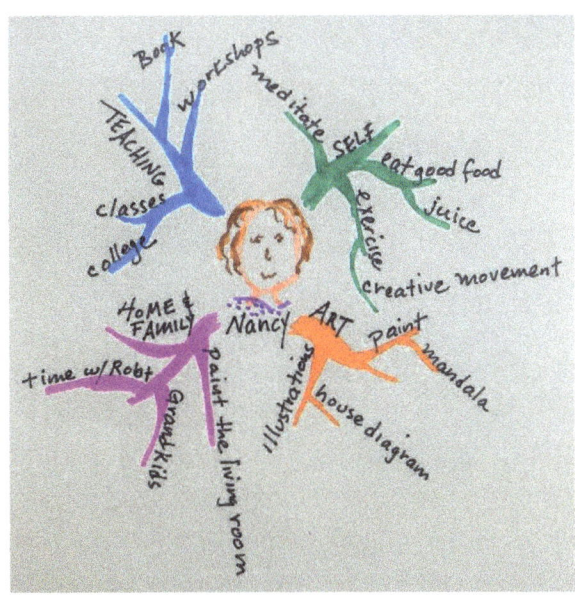

1. Start with the topic at the center. You can start with yourself for your initial mind map.

2. Now using a different color for each branch emanating from the center, starting with a thicker line which tapers as you move outwards, brainstorm the areas of your life. Remember, try to keep them simple. You'll be adding thinner branches to these to describe more of the details.

3. The extending branches can go on indefinitely, but you'll know when you have enough.

The same technique can be applied to more specific topics. For example, if someone is contemplating finding or creating a new job or career, that can go in the center. Then the branches will be the talents and skills they have, or the various possibilities for work which call for those talents and skills. Remember, as with the house diagram, this is *your* mind map – there's no right way to do it, only your way.

## Synthesis

To me, synthesis is like integration, but there's a slight shift in the interaction of the parts with the whole. In integration, some of the parts may interact as I've described above. But what happens when ALL the aspects of oneself are combined into one functional whole? My guides have challenged me with this idea because it is where we as humans are moving, part of our ascension or evolution to a higher level of awareness. Wholeness is often spoken of as a goal in our self-realization. We need to accept ALL of ourselves, not just what we perceive as the good or 'light' parts. We are multi-dimensional beings. We experience a full range of emotions, not just the positive ones. I tend to avoid using the term 'negative emotion' since it implies that these more difficult or challenging emotions like grief, sadness, anger, or frustration should be avoided.

By acknowledging that we feel that way, we can process those feelings (for example, through Expressive Arts), and come to terms with them. We learn to accept every aspect of our personality and experience. Sometimes this requires compassion towards ourselves. We are a work in progress, and no matter how we wish for perfection, that just ain't gonna happen.

Now imagine, you are a fully integrated being – you've acknowledged your flaws and valued your best qualities. There is a sense of self-acceptance, a sense of well-being that comes from this. Now go one step further, as we will soon be asked to do. Be all your aspects all at the same time! Your parts function together simultaneously all the time. This means I am spiritual being, teacher, and artist (not to mention wife, mother, grandmother, and friend) all at once.

I was sitting in morning meditation one day, thinking about my three self-portraits (*Gloria Caelesti, Stella Spiralus,* and *Spiritus*). All were received and named in meditation, one after the other, in that order: spiritual being, teacher, and artist. All three of these threads developed simultaneously over the course of years. They weren't three separate lives – they were all parts of this one lifetime (and probably many others as well). I felt my guides were asking me to not live them separately – one at a time, but simultaneously. As I sat there, I imagined what would happen if the three images were overlaid photographically – what kind of an image would emerge? As I mentally placed one on top of the other, each slightly transparent to reveal the others, I had a very sudden experience: a shamanic being dressed in white bird feathers appeared and stabbed me in the breast with their sword. I had an immediate jolt of pain, which then disappeared as quickly as the image had appeared to me. Why a white bird? I'd been having visions of white birds recently – actual birds, not a human form dressed as bird. Was this a healing vision – more than a vision because I felt that very real stab of pain? This might seem frightening to some people, but perhaps because I was in a meditative state, I was experiencing it without attachment, and I trust in Guidance, knowing I am protected, knowing I am guided, knowing I am blessed.

Winternight Trinity overlay

My most recent attempts at house diagrams have surprised me. About a year ago, it resulted in a yin/yang of self and others. I understood from this that whatever I do for my own development and self-expression was on one side but balanced by what I do to support others' development and self-expression. I didn't need to go any further. I simply knew. More recently, it came out in the formation of a 5-pointed star – each point labeled with the categories incorporated in former house diagrams, though slightly altered (five now, not the previous four): Spiritual, Healing (self), Art, Home & Family, and Teaching, with a spiral at the center indicating that they are all happening simultaneously. This diagram comprises more of my soul energy – my wholeness or sense of Oneness. All this is labeled as being supported by, yes, balance, integration, and synthesis. Just as these visuals can be line drawings/diagrams, they can also be pieces of art, using any combination of media. This serves to bring the evolution to light, grounding the energy into form.

Now that this series of energy mandalas is complete – and that's how it felt, once I'd reached the twelfth large canvas, I feel as though I am being guided to continue this process of bringing the higher-level energies into form in an accessible way to others. This still incorporates the experience of meditation – it is so much a part of who I am, that it will follow me anywhere. I do feel as though my intuitive abilities, including my capacity to draw divine, celestial light into my body and put it into physical form, have increased manyfold. It's so much a part of my waking state – a steadiness, an anchoring, in something deeper and heart-centered. If anything, this time has been a realization of soul essence. There is no denying our divine identity. Step into that.

And so, I leave you with these insights and tools for your own use, hopefully empowering you to live your own process of spiritual evolution in a creative way. You have a fully operating inner guidance system – it's up to you to attune to it, clear it if necessary, and allow the guidance to come through. Trust that your own intuition will take you there. May you find the wholeness you desire, the sense of Oneness with All, and the clarity to decipher it. Once the journey begins, you can't go back. You can stop and rest along the way, but the process of unfoldment has begun.

## Channeling

*Blessings. We are here with you at this time. We identify ourselves as The Ones, for we are many entities working together, supporting, fostering, the enlightenment, the raising of vibration on your planet Earth at this time. Many of you are aware of the ascension energies which are pouring forth upon your planet at this time. We wish you to know that this is proceeding quite well. And the shadow you are perceiving which can feel quite intense right now with your pandemic, the underside of humanity being revealed in what we would say are disturbing ways, for darkness is still upon the planet. There is a wholeness, however, and so we see that there is as much Light coming in your energy field as there is darkness. The Light will uncover the shadow and reveal it. However, we do not wish you to feel as though you are overwhelmed by this shadow life, for it is dissipating. It is dissolving. And as it comes to the surface and is revealed, it is released. You let it go. You do not cling to it as if it were reality. Instead, we ask that you ground the new energies coming into your atmosphere at this time. And what does that mean to ground the energy? It simply means to put it into form, to live it in your daily life. This may mean being creative in your own individual way and seeing ways in which you can co-create a new vision, a new reality of what will come to pass on Earth. It is up to you in your individual lives to develop that sense of Light, to embody that sense of Light. And so we would ask of you at this time to use practices such as meditation to bring in that Light and to pursue your creative endeavors, whether they be in the artistic field, the musical field, the dramatic field, or perhaps there is another way that you feel creative. However, it is essential at this time that you, each and every one of you, find YOUR path to expressing that creativity in its fullest sense and then we can, you see, begin to rebuild upon this planet, which is now undergoing a major, yes, major shift, a major transformation. Your endeavors will allow that energy to come through, for you will in that sense be bringing through the Light and be putting it into form.*

*And we thank you, we thank you from the bottoms of our hearts, for we have been pursuing this ascension energy for some time now, as many of you are aware. And now is the EXACT MOMENT when this all comes to pass. And it is so,*

*SO very essential, at this particular time that you envelop yourself in that shifting energy which is moving upwards and downwards in the Light. For we say downwards because you are bringing down-wards this extraordinary rising Light. So you see that there is a simultaneous movement of energy upwards and downwards as this shift takes place. And so again we thank you for your participation. It is treasured. We honor you with all our being. Now some of you will know the names of Archangel Michael, beloved Archangel Metatron, and our Sananda. We are participating in this transformation. We honor you. We thank you. And we bless you. Go in peace.*

The Ones

## Gratitude

I want to thank The Ones, who have supported and encouraged me in this process of my unfoldment: My playful angelic guides and Archangel Michael, who have guided and protected me; Archangel Metatron, who has sent me an infusion of Light and invaluable information; and Sananda, who has opened my heart to hold the Light of Oneness.[13] I am eternally grateful. Heartfelt thanks to Baba Muktananda and Gurumayi Chidvilasananda, as well as all my guides and teachers. I now begin a new cycle, not only because of my own soul's evolution, but because collectively, we have entered an extraordinary new time. My latest directive: *paint crystalline light*. This should be fun...

---

[13] The Ones: Archangel Michael is known as a Protector of Humanity, depicted with sword and shield to fight against darkness. Archangel Metatron is Keeper of the Akashic Records, known to bring increasing levels of light energy, sitting by the throne of the Divine. Sananda is the soul level of Jesus, an ascended master associated with the Sacred Heart.

*Winternight, 8x8, acrylic on canvas*

*I believe to the core of my being, that when we are fully functional, we have enormous creative capacities to manifest an amazing world. My personal role in this life is to encourage people to see they are an integral part of the whole, that their self-expression is essential to the process of transformation on a global and Universal level.*

~Nancy Winternight

# 6
## The Energy Mandalas

Having already discussed the process of receiving the images for these paintings in Chapter 1, there is little left to say, except that they were received in the order presented here. Although I have seen energy mandalas in meditation since this time, they have not been as distinct as these twelve were, nor have they been accompanied by any directives as these were. It's as if to the Ones were saying, 'we need you to paint these twelve and no more.' Metatron was especially involved in delivering the images to me. I have done my best to present them as perceived, and according to the directions provided. I am delighted to present them here.

Sacred Geometry 2020

Merkabah 2020

Color is Everything					2020

Activation Codes 2020

Healing the Heart — 2021

Shakti 2021

Intuition 2021

Guidance 2021

Creativity 2021

Soul Traveler (Wormhole) — 2021

Return to the Central Sun　　　　　　　　　　　　　　　　　　　　　　　　　　2021

Soul Map (Nova Emerging) 2021

Nancy Winternight is an artist, teacher, and spiritual counselor who teaches Expressive Arts, offering women's groups and private sessions. She lives just outside of the infamous Woodstock, NY. You can reach her at: www.nancywinternight.com

www.ingramcontent.com/pod-product-compliance
Lightning Source LLC
Chambersburg PA
CBHW060921170426
43191CB00024B/2449